The History

and

Present State

of

Virginia

American
History
Landmarks

Edited by
David Freeman Hawke

Robert Beverley

The History

and

Present State

of

Virginia

A Selection

The Bobbs-Merrill Company, Inc.
Indianapolis & New York

Robert Beverley, 1673–1722
The History and Present State of Virginia
was first published in 1705.

F
229
.B593
1971

Contents

Introduction

1

A danger confronts the enthusiast who wants to persuade friends to read Robert Beverley's *History of Virginia*. The urge persists to talk about the book as a significant historical document, a classic of American literature, or a pioneering study for anthropologists and naturalists. It is all these things, but such labels make the *History* something less than it is. Out of a blend of love and wrath—love for Virginia, wrath for the lies perpetrated about it in England—Beverley produced one of the liveliest, wittiest, and best written accounts we have of life in colonial America. He sought, so he said, to give readers "a tolerable entertainment." Contemporaries on the receiving end of his barbs may have questioned the entertaining quality of the book, but modern readers never have. It remains as readable today as in 1705 when it was published.

Those who have little taste for history should not be put off by the title. In lesser hands a survey of Virginia's early past, of its natural endowments, its Indians, and its government could be as tedious as a treasurer's report. Beverley is too much engaged with his subject, too opinionated and injudicious to be dull. He savors whatever at the moment engages him. "I have set in the shade at the heads of the rivers angling," he confesses, "and spent as much time in taking the fish off the hook as in waiting for their taking it." An earthy sense of humor impels him to go out of the way to tease a prudish friend with a flower that "resembled the pudenda of a man and woman lovingly joined in one." He gives as much space to a game played between hawk and eagle—the hawk with a captured fish loiters in the air waiting for an eagle to give chase, and if none appears he makes "a saucy noise" to attract an antagonist and get the game under way—as he does to an Indian massacre. A fight between a dog and a rattlesnake over a squirrel intrigues him as much as the machinations of a royal governor.

His curiosity knows no bounds. Though an honorable man, he admits at one time to breaking into an Indian house of worship to see an idol up close; at another, to plying a native with liquor in order to persuade him to talk about his religious beliefs.

Beverley reveals as much of himself as he does of Virginia in the book. He lived as a member of the élite in a tight little provincial society and knew that outspokenness would win only reproof from the Establishment, yet he would always be himself. He misses no chance to flail compatriots who "sponge upon the blessings of a warm sun and a fruitful soil." At a time when it was unfashionable to do so, he heaped praise on the former royal governor, Sir William Berkeley (the book's hero); he also castigated the current governor, Sir Francis Nicholson (the villain), knowing that Nicholson could, as he did, ruin him politically. He even dared to make Opechancanough, the Indian chief who had directed two great massacres against Virginians and nearly exterminated the colony, something of a tragic hero, still arrogant and defiant even in captivity, though grown so old and decrepit he could not walk and could only see when servants lifted up his heavy eyelids.

Beverley reveals himself to be more than a contented and curious man. He was the first in the century since Jamestown's settlement who dared or cared to brag openly of his American background, a bold act in an age when Virginians aped English fashions and society and filled their houses with imports from the mother country. When Beverley speaks of "my country," as he often does, he means Virginia, not England. He discovered that new breed of man, the American, some seventy years before Crèvecoeur revealed him to the world. Those who had written earlier of the American experience, like John Winthrop or William Bradford, reflected the thought of Englishmen overseas. They wrote about America as later Englishmen would write about India and Africa. The style and content of Beverley's *History* were as American as, say, Mark Twain's *Life on the Mississippi*.

The allusion to Twain's work is not far-fetched. Beverley's book *is* a landmark in American literature, the fountainhead, so to speak, from which have sprung volumes like *Life on the Mississippi*. Twain held much in common with Beverley, even though he never heard of the gentleman. Both chose to write in the American vernacular, although Beverley felt the need to apologize for the plainness of his literary "dress" by saying, "I am an Indian and don't pretend to be exact in my language." Twain on Negroes matches Beverley on Indians in the attempt to avoid platitudes and stereotypes. Both see their countries as latter-day Edens, but they seek to depict them as they are. Twain shows the Mississippi on a summer morning with the mist curling off the water, while a cool breeze carries onto the river the smell of woods and flowers, but also the stink of dead fish that have washed up on shore. Beverley admits after an exuberant description of his Garden that it is also inhabited by mosquitoes, bugs that lurk in the bedding, seedticks, red worms, and snakes. Both, for all their effort to be truthful, lapse occasionally into exaggeration. Beverley most notably does so when speaking of bullfrogs, so called "from the roaring they make"; these can sometimes be found so large that six Frenchmen might make "a comfortable meal of its carcass." (Beverley eliminated this whopper from his second edition, which suggests that he did not exaggerate for the sake of humor.) If it can be said American literature was conceived with William Bradford's *Of Plymouth Plantation* and came of age with Mark Twain's work, then let it be said that it was born with Robert Beverley's *History*.

2

Beverley, like Twain, aimed "to say nothing but the naked truth," but the truth he perceived, at least on political matters, mainly reflected the views of his father, Major Robert Beverley. Though Beverley was thirty-two when he published the *History*, and his father had been dead eight years, the major seems to have continued from the grave to shape his son's judgments.

Major Beverley had emigrated from comfortable circumstances in Yorkshire to Virginia in 1663. He brought with him enough capital to buy a farm already carved from the wilderness and enough ability and energy to become one of the colony's richest planters—by the time of his death he had accumulated forty-two slaves and some fifty thousand acres of land—as well as a power in politics. From an early appointment as justice of the peace, he moved on to become clerk of the House of Burgesses, and finally a member of the Council, a post handed to him by Governor Berkeley during Bacon's Rebellion, when the major emerged as one of the governor's staunchest supporters. Major Beverley apparently enjoyed himself in the rebellion. It ended, he was quoted as saying, before he had "plundered enough," a remark, it might be added, possibly aired when in his cups, for according to a friend "when so taken he is not *compos mentis*."

After the rebellion the major directed his antagonism against the string of royal governors who followed Berkeley, none of whom he approved of and all of whom are censured in his son's book. He was a vigorous defender of the power of the House of Burgesses, to such an extent that he was soon judged a man of "evil fame" and removed from the Council. Governor Culpeper restored him to his seat on the Council (which may explain the moderate and balanced account of that most notorious of Virginia's governors in the *History*), but the major continued to provoke the Establishment. He was imprisoned in 1682 for being a "prime actor" in a movement to raise tobacco prices by burning the plants of those who refused to cut back production. After two years in and out of prison defending himself against a variety of charges, some of them trumped up, he finally submitted to the humiliation of appearing before the Council on bended knee to ask its forgiveness. The act may have broken his spirit. He died three years later, in 1687, without making a further stir on the political scene.

Robert Beverley, the second son of nine children, was born in 1673. He was sent as a boy to school in England and remained there until he was about nineteen. Soon after returning home he began to accumulate the knowledge of Virginia government he displays in the *History*. He started as a volunteer clerk in the office of the colony's secretary of state, and from there advanced to become clerk of the Committee of Public Claims, then clerk of the general court, clerk of the Council, and finally, clerk of the General Assembly. In 1697 he married perhaps the richest girl in Virginia, Ursula Byrd, the sixteen-year-old daughter of William Byrd I. (He may have met his wife in England, where she had been sent at the age of four to be educated; she returned to Virginia the year of her marriage to Beverley.) She died in childbirth, less than a year after the wedding. The son survived; Beverley never remarried.

By 1700 Beverley had become one of the colony's eminent citizens. He lived in Jamestown, at the center of Virginia's social and political life, and served as the town's representative in the House. His holdings in land were scattered throughout the colony, and he missed no chance to augment what he had gained from his marriage and inherited from his father. Along with his father's political opinions, he appears also to have inherited the major's truculence. It was a rare court session that failed to find Beverley's name on the docket, usually in regard to a dispute over land. A decision that deprived him of title to one of his largest holdings angered him enough to go to England in 1705 to plead his case before the Privy Council.

The year and a half Beverley spent in England proved momentous for him in several ways. He lost the suit before the Privy Council, and he also undercut all future chance for any political or financial plums the governor might hand out by writing indiscreet letters to friends back home. He said that in reports to the Crown, Governor Nicholson and Robert Quarry, the surveyor general (and soon to become one of the minor villains in the *History*), had slandered Virginia's leading citizens, among them his father-in-law, calling them "obstinate people of Commonwealth principles." The reports, said Beverley, called members of the Council vain and cowardly and those of the House unthinking and willful. And, he added, "it's laid as a crime of them [in the House] that they think themselves entitled to the liberties of Englishmen." Worst of all, according to Beverley, the Duke (Beverley's nickname for Nicholson) wanted to erect a standing army in America. (This fear of a standing army accounts for the warm and exaggerated praise of the local militia's virtues in the *History*.)

Nicholson exploded when he got a glimpse of these remarks; Beverley, he suggested, should "get himself close-shaved" and apply for admission to one of her Majesty's insane asylums, "and there he may meet with real chains instead of imaginary ones that I was preparing for her Majesty's loyal and dutiful subjects of Virginia." Having spoken, Nicholson acted—by removing Beverley from his most lucrative clerkship.

If the letters home had not been enough to put Beverley outside the Establishment—which they were—the third event of his stay in England would have completed the job. This was the publication of his *History and Present State of Virginia*.

3

The reasons why men endure the agony of writing books vary with the men. Beverley said his *History* resulted from a request by an English bookseller to look over a manuscript on Virginia. He found the account filled with "prodigious phantasms" and far "too faulty and too imperfect to be mended." This censorious judgment may have been influenced by the knowledge that his brother-in-law William Byrd II, whom he despised for his eager chase after status in English society, had helped shape the manuscript. Publicly, however, he only said it grieved him to see "so fine a country . . . so misrepresented to the common people of England." He determined to set matters straight with his own report.

No doubt other less ingenuous motives fixed his decision. Beverley had been collecting material about Virginia for years, and the fact that he brought his bundle of notes to England suggests that he had given thought to a book before leaving home. A desire to take revenge upon those who had oppressed his father may have been one reason for him to write the *History*. He may have wanted also to educate the British government, hoping that a better understanding of American conditions might lead to wiser rule by the Crown. Finally, he wished to attract emigrants to Virginia from among the "common people of England" as well as from among the oppressed Huguenots on the Continent. (A French translation of the book went through four printings, three originating in Holland, one in France.) William Penn's recent success in directing the migrating stream from Europe toward his "holy experiment" had distressed Virginians, and Beverley clearly hoped his book would help divert some of the flow toward his country.

Regardless of why Beverley produced the *History*, one thing is clear: writing the book exposed a contradiction in his ideas about Virginia. A dilemma he seemed unable to resolve emerged from the opening pages. The dilemma was this: how can civilized man live in Eden without being corrupted by it? Some travelers had viewed Virginia as a hostile and howling wilderness filled with maurauding savages, but Beverley sided with those who found the country "so agreeable that paradise itself seemed to be there in its first native luster." Virginia began as a land of "purity and plenty"; somewhere along the way the purity vanished and the plenty diminished. In the historical chapters of the book Beverley implies that the blame for soiling his Paradise should fall on the string of corrupt and misguided royal officials who tried to foist "English fopperies" upon an American pattern. Sir William Berkeley alone stands forth as a governor "who was always contriving and industrious for the good of the country."

The dilemma becomes clearer to the modern reader, if not to Beverley, in the chapters on the Indians and their culture. Beverley admires the Indians because "they seemed not debauched nor corrupted with those pomps and vanities which had depraved and enslaved the rest of mankind." Before the English came they lived "happy, I think, in their simple state of nature and in their enjoyment of plenty without the curse of labor." The English corrupted them. "They have introduced drunkenness and luxury amongst them, which have multiplied their wants and put them upon desiring a thousand things they never dreamt of before."

The white man has corrupted Paradise, but what has Paradise done to the white man? The abundance has led him, Beverley admits, to "sponge upon the blessings of a warm sun and a fruitful soil and almost grutch the pains of gathering in the bounties of the earth." Englishmen accustomed at home to a life of discipline and work, says Beverley, in Virginia have become slothful and indolent. Beverley ends with the hope his book "will rouse them out of their lethargy and excite them to make the most of all those happy advantages which nature has given them."

Professor Leo Marx has argued in a perceptive essay in *The Machine in the Garden* that Beverley fails to extricate himself from the dilemma he has raised. What Beverley wanted but saw no way to achieve, Professor Marx says, "was to reconcile his admiration for the primitive life with what he knew of the needs of a truly civilized community." Actually, Beverley not only saw the dilemma but resolved it—personally at least—in the life he shaped for himself after he arrived back in Virginia.

When he returned, Beverley abandoned Jamestown to settle on his plantation, Beverley Park, in King and Queen County. He sat for his county in the House of Burgesses in 1706, then retired to his plantation to live out the remaining sixteen years of his life as a spectator of politics. He did as much as a wealthy man could to duplicate the simple and moderate life of the Indians he had praised in the *History*. His remark, "I am an Indian," now applied to more than his literary style. He lived comfortably, a visitor to Beverley Park remarked, but with "nothing in or about his house but what is necessary." Guests slept in decent beds, but in rooms unadorned with curtains or drapes. Wooden stools built from local lumber, rather than fashionable cane chairs imported from England, served as seats. Travelers drank wine made from grapes grown on the plantation. "He lives upon the product of his land," the visitor concluded.

Beverley turned his back on politics but not society. He enjoyed the pleasure of fishing and hunting and exploring the countryside in his leisure, but he did not abjure his responsibilities as a citizen. He struck up a friendship and performed several minor services for Governor Alexander Spotswood, who came to Virginia in 1710 and became during his twelve years there the single royal official Beverley regarded with respect. To wean Virginians from a to-bacco economy he experimented, as had Governor Berkeley before him, with the growing of grapes, going so far as to bet neighbors he could produce seven hundred gallons of wine in seven years. (He stood to win, at odds of ten to one, one thousand guineas; the outcome of the bet is not known.) Beverley completed his public service to Virginia in 1722, the year of his death, with two books—one a new edition of the *History* (a product of a mellowed spirit and in almost every way inferior to the first ver-sion), the other *An Abridgement of the Public Laws of Virginia*, a handy compendium of Virginia (not English) legislation for neophyte justices of the peace. He gracefully thanked the Crown in his Preface for at last sending over the able Governor Spots-wood, whose presence, he said, had brought the "greatest hap-piness that ever befell Virginia, raising it from need and indigence to a flourishing plenty and prosperity, with an increase of virtue and good manners." The thanks he gave Spotswood might equally well have been given by Virginia to its censorious but loyal and enthusiastic son, Robert Beverley.

D. F. H.

Note on the Text

Thanks to Louis B. Wright, Robert Beverley's *History* in its most acidulous and sparkling form has been accessible to colonial historians for over twenty years. Mr. Wright in 1947 edited the first reprinting of this "ingenuous, vigorous, wonderfully vivid book" since its original publication nearly two and a half centuries earlier. He had the good sense to ignore Beverley's second, emasculated edition of 1722. (Those interested in a comparison of the two editions should see Mr. Wright's Introduction to his edition, as well as his Appendix with a page-by-page list of the changes.)

This edition of the *History* does not supplant Mr. Wright's reproduction of the original. It is designed for students and laymen. To that end spellings and punctuation have been modernized, and Beverley's numerous contractions expanded, except with such words as " 'em," " 'tis," and "tho'," which have been retained to keep the flavor of the informal style. Excisions have been few, totaling less than one-tenth of the text and limited largely to repetitious material or lengthy quotations from secondary sources, particularly John Smith's *General History*.

The History
and
Present State
of
Virginia

Preface

'Tis agreed that travelers are of all men the most suspected of insincerity. This does not only hold in their private conversations, but likewise in the grand tours and travels with which they pester the public and break the bookseller. There are no books (the legends of the saints always excepted) so stuffed with poetical stories as voyages, and the more distant the countries lie which they pretend to describe, the greater the license those privileged authors take in imposing upon the world. The French travels are commonly more infamous on this account than any other, which must be imputed to the strong genius of that nation to hyperbole and romance. They are fond of dressing up everything in their gay fashion, from a happy opinion that their own fopperies make any subject more entertaining. The English, it must be granted, invent more within the compass of probability and are contented to be less ornamental while they are more sincere.

I make no question, but the following account will come in for its share of this imputation. I shall be reputed as arrant a traveler as the rest, and my credit (like that of women) will be condemned for the sins of my company. However, I entreat the gentle reader to be so just as not to convict me upon bare suspicion; let the evidence be plain, or at least amount to a violent presumption, and then I don't fear being acquitted. If an honest author might be believed in his own case, I would solemnly declare that I have not knowingly asserted any untrue thing in the whole book. On the contrary, I fear I shall rather be accused of saying too much truth than too little. If I have had the misfortune to have erred in any particular way, which yet I have used all imaginable care to avoid, I hope the world with all its uncharitableness will vouchsafe to forgive my understanding.

If I might be so happy as to settle my credit with the reader, the next favor I would ask of him should be not to criticize too unmercifully upon my style. I am an Indian and don't pretend to be exact in my language. But I hope the plainness of my dress will

3

give him the kinder impressions of my honesty, which is what I pretend to. Truth desires only to be understood and never affects the reputation of being finely equipped. It depends upon its own intrinsic value and, like beauty, is rather concealed than set off by ornament.

I wonder nobody has ever presented the world with a tolerable account of our plantations. Nothing of that kind has yet appeared, except some few general descriptions that have been calculated more for the benefit of the bookseller than for the information of mankind. If I may judge of the rest by what has been published concerning Virginia, I will take the liberty to say there's none of 'em either true or so much as well invented. Such accounts are as impertinent as ill pictures that resemble anybody as much as the persons they are drawn for. For my part, I have endeavored to hit the likeness, though perhaps my coloring may not have all the life and beauty I could wish.

BOOK ONE

The History of the First Settlement
of Virginia and the Government
Thereof to the Present Time

1

Showing What Happened in the First Attempts
to Settle Virginia Before
the Discovery of Chesapeake Bay

The learned and valiant Sir Walter Raleigh having entertained
some deeper and more serious considerations upon the state of
the earth than most other men of his time, as may sufficiently
appear by his incomparable book, *The History of the World*, and
having laid together the many stories then in Europe concerning
America—the native beauty, riches, and value of this part of the
world, and the immense profits the Spaniards drew from a small
settlement or two thereon made—resolved upon an adventure for
further discoveries.

According to this purpose, in the year of our Lord, 1583, he got
several men of great value and estate to join with him in an expedition of this nature. And for their encouragement obtained
letters patents from Queen Elizabeth bearing date the 25th of
March, 1584, for turning their discoveries to their own advantage.

In April following they set out two small vessels under the
command of Captain Philip Amadas and Captain Arthur Barlow,
who, after a prosperous voyage, anchored at the inlet by Roanoke,
at present under the government of North Carolina. They made
good profit of the Indian truck, which they bought for things of

much inferior value, and returned. Being over-pleased with their profits and finding all things there entirely new and surprising, they gave a very advantageous account of matters by representing the country so delightful and desirable, so pleasant and plentiful; the climate and air so temperate, sweet, and wholesome; the woods and soil so charming and fruitful; and all other things so agreeable that paradise itself seemed to be there in its first native luster.

And to make it yet more desirable, they reported the native Indians (which were then the only inhabitants) so affable, kind and good-natured; so uncultivated in learning, trades, and fashion; so innocent and ignorant of all manner of politics, tricks, and cunning; and so desirous of the company of the English that they seemed rather to be like soft wax, ready to take any impression than any ways likely to oppose the settling of the English near them. They represented it as a scene laid open for the good and gracious Queen Elizabeth to propagate the Gospel in and extend her dominions over, as if purposely reserved for her Majesty by a peculiar direction of providence that had brought all former adventurers in this affair to nothing. And to give a further taste of their discovery, they took with them in their return for England two men of the native Indians, named Wanchese and Manteo.

Her Majesty accordingly took the hint and espoused the project, as far as her present engagements in war with Spain would let her. Being so well pleased with the account given that as the greatest mark of honor she could do the discovery she called the country by the name of Virginia; as well for that it was first discovered in her reign, a virgin queen, as that it did still seem to retain the virgin purity and plenty of the first creation and the people their primitive innocence.

This was encouragement enough for a new adventure and set people's invention at work till they had satisfied themselves and made sufficient essays for the further discovery of the country. Pursuant whereunto Sir Richard Grenville, the chief of Sir Walter Raleigh's associates, having obtained seven sail of ships well laden with provision, arms, ammunition, and spare men to make a settlement, set out in person with them early in the spring of the succeeding year to make further discoveries, taking back the two Indians with him. And according to his wish, in the latter end of May, arrived at the same place where the English had been the year before. There he made a settlement, sowed beans and peas, which he saw come up and grow to admiration while he stayed, which was about two months. And having made some little discoveries more in the sound to the southward and got some treasure in skins, furs, pearl, and other rarities of the country for things of inconsiderable value, he returned for England, leaving 108 men upon Roanoke Island under the command of Mr. Ralph Lane to keep possession.

As soon as Sir Richard Grenville was gone, they, according to order and their own inclination, set themselves earnestly about discovering the country and ranged about a little too indiscreetly up the rivers and into the land backward from the rivers, which gave the Indians a jealousy of their meaning. For they cut off several stragglers of them and had laid designs to destroy the rest, but were happily prevented. This put the English upon the precaution of keeping more within bounds and not venturing themselves too defenseless abroad, who till then had depended too much upon the natives' simplicity and innocence.

After the Indians had done this mischief, they never observed any real faith towards those English. For being naturally suspicious and revengeful themselves, they never thought the English could forgive them; and so by this jealousy caused by the cowardice of their nature they were continually doing mischief.

The English, notwithstanding all this, continued their discoveries, but more carefully than they had done before, and kept the Indians in some awe by threatening them with the return of their companions again with a greater supply of men and goods. And before the cold of the winter became uneasy, they had extended their discoveries near a hundred miles along the seacoast to the northward; but not reaching the southern cape of Chesapeake Bay in Virginia, they had as yet found no good harbor.

In this condition they maintained their settlement all the winter and till August following, but were much distressed for want of provisions, not having conveniences like them of taking fish and fowl. Besides, being now fallen out with the Indians, they feared to expose themselves to their contempt and cruelty because they had not received the supply they talked of and which had been expected in the spring.

All they could do under these distresses and the despair of the recruits promised them this year was only to keep a good looking out to seaward, if perchance they might find any means of escape or recruit. And to their great joy and satisfaction, in August aforesaid they happened to espy and make themselves be seen to Sir Francis Drake's fleet, consisting of twenty-three sail, who being sent by her Majesty upon the coast of America in search of the Spanish treasures had orders from her Majesty to take a view of this plantation and see what assistance or encouragement it wanted. Their first petition to him was to grant them a fresh supply of men and provisions with a small vessel and boats to attend them; that so if they should be put to distress for want of relief they might embark for England. This was as readily granted by Sir Francis Drake as asked by them, and a ship was appointed them, which ship they began immediately to fit up and supply plentifully with all manner of stores for a long stay. But while they were adoing this, a great storm arose and drove that very ship (with some others) from her anchor to sea, and so she was lost for that occasion.

Sir Francis would have given them another ship, but this accident coming on the back of so many hardships which they had undergone daunted them and put them upon imagining that providence was averse to their design. And now having given over for that year the expectation of their promised supply from England, they consulted together and agreed to desire Sir Francis Drake to take them along with him, which he did.

Thus their first intention of settlement fell, after discovering many things of the natural growth of the country useful for the life of man and beneficial to trade; they having observed a vast variety of fish, fowl, and beasts; fruits, seeds, plants, roots, timber-trees, sweet-woods, and gums. They had likewise attained some little knowledge in the language of the Indians, their religion, manners, and ways of correspondence one with another, and been made sensible of their cunning and treachery towards themselves.

While these things were thus acting in America, the adventurers in England were providing, tho' too tediously, to send them recruits. And tho' it was late before they could dispatch them (for they met with several disappointments and had many squabbles among themselves), however, at last they provided four good ships with all manner of recruits suitable for the colony, and Sir Walter Raleigh designed to go in person with them.

Sir Walter got his ship ready first, and fearing the ill consequence of a delay and the discouragement it might be to those that were left to make a settlement, he set sail by himself. And a fortnight after him Sir Richard Grenville sailed with the three other ships.

Sir Walter fell in with the land at Cape Hatteras, a little to the southward of the place where the 108 men had been settled, and after search not finding them he returned. However, Sir Richard, with his ships, found the place where he had left the men, but entirely deserted, which was at first a great disheartening to him, thinking them all destroyed, because he knew not that Sir Francis Drake had been there and taken them off. But he was a little better satisfied by Manteo's report that they were not cut off by the Indians, tho' he could give no good account what was become of them. However, notwithstanding this seeming discouragement, he again left fifty men in the same island of Roanoke, built them houses necessary, gave them two years' provision, and returned.

The next summer, being anno 1587, three ships more were sent under the command of Mr. John White, who himself was to settle there as governor, with more men and some women, carrying also plentiful recruits of provisions.

In the latter end of July they arrived at Roanoke aforesaid, where they again encountered the uncomfortable news of the loss of these men also; who (as they were informed by Manteo) were secretly set upon by the Indians, some cut off, and the others fled and not to be heard of, and their place of habitation now all grown up with weeds. However, they repaired the houses on Roanoke and sat down there again.

The 13th of August they christened Manteo and styled him Lord of Dassamonpeak, an Indian nation so called, in reward of the fidelity he had shown to the English from the beginning; who being the first Indian that was made a Christian in that part of the world, I thought it not amiss to remember him.

On the same occasion also may be mentioned the first child there born of Christian parentage, viz., a daughter of Mr. Ananias Dare. She was born the 18th of the same August upon Roanoke, and after the name of the country was christened Virginia.

This seemed to be a settlement prosperously made, being carried on with much zeal and unanimity among themselves. The form of government consisted of a governor and twelve councilors, incorporated by the name of the governor and assistants of the city of Raleigh in Virginia.

Many nations of the Indians renewed their peace and made firm leagues with the corporation. The chief men of the English also were so far from being disheartened at the former disappointments that they disputed for the liberty of remaining on the spot, and by mere constraint compelled Mr. White, their governor, to return for England to negotiate the business of their recruits and supply, as a man the most capable to manage that affair, leaving at his departure 115 in the corporation.

It was above two years before Mr. White could obtain any grant of supplies; and then in the latter end of the year 1589 he set out from Plymouth with three ships and sailed round by the western and Caribbean islands, they having hitherto not found any nearer way. For tho' they were skilled in navigation and understood the use of the globes, yet did example so much prevail upon them that they chose to sail a thousand leagues about rather than attempt a more direct passage.

Towards the middle of August, 1590, they arrived upon the coast at Cape Hatteras and went to search upon Roanoke for the people; but found by letters on the trees that they were removed to Croatan, one of the islands forming the sound and southward of Roanoke about twenty leagues, but no sign of distress. Thither they designed to sail to them in their ships, but a storm arising in the meanwhile lay so hard upon them that their cables broke; they lost three of their anchors, were forced to sea, and so returned home without ever going near those poor people again for sixteen years following. And it is supposed that the Indians, seeing them forsaken by their country and unfurnished of their expected supplies, cut them off. For to this day they were never more heard of.

2

Containing an Account of the First Settlement of Chesapeake Bay in Virginia by the Corporation of London Adventurers, and Their Proceedings During Their Government by a President and Council Elective

The merchants of London, Bristol, Exeter, and Plymouth soon perceived what great gains might be made of a trade this way if it were well managed and colonies could be rightly settled; which was sufficiently evinced by the great profits some ships had made which had not met with ill accidents. Encouraged by this prospect, they joined together in a petition to King James the First showing forth that it would be too much for any single person to attempt the settling of colonies and to carry on so considerable a trade. They therefore prayed his Majesty to incorporate them and enable them to raise a joint stock for that purpose and to countenance their undertaking.

His Majesty did accordingly grant their petition, and by letters patents bearing date the 10th of April, 1606, did in one patent incorporate them into two distinct companies and make two separate colonies.

By virtue of this patent, Captain John Smith was [one of those] sent by the London Company in December, 1606, on his voyage with three small ships. And the first place they landed upon was the southern cape of that Bay which they named Cape Henry and the northern Cape Charles in honor of the king's two eldest sons; and the first great river they searched, whose Indian name was Powhatan, they called James River after the king's own name.

Before they would make any settlement here, they made a full search of James River, and then by unanimous consent pitched upon a peninsula about fifty miles up the river, which, besides the goodness of the soil, was esteemed as most fit and capable to be made a place both of trade and security—two-thirds thereof being environed by the main river, which affords good anchorage all along, and the other third by a small narrow river capable of receiving many vessels of a hundred ton, quite up as high as till it meets within thirty yards of the main river again, and where generally in spring tides it overflows into the main river. By which means the land they chose to pitch their town upon has obtained the name of an island. In this back river ships and small vessels may ride lashed to one another and moored ashore secure from all wind and weather whatsoever.

The town as well as the river had the honor to be called by King James's name. The whole island thus enclosed contains about two thousand acres of high land and several thousand of very good and firm marsh and is an extraordinary good pasture as any in that country.

By means of the narrow passage this place was of great security to them from the Indian enemy. And if they had then known of the biting of the worm in the salts, they would have valued this place upon that account also as being free from that mischief.

They were no sooner settled in all this happiness and security but they fell into jars and dissensions among themselves, by a greedy grasping at the Indian treasures envying and overreaching one another in that trade.

After five weeks' stay before this town, the ships returned home again leaving 108 men settled in the form of government before spoken of.

After the ships were gone, the same sort of feuds and disorders happened continually among them, to the unspeakable damage of the plantation.

The Indians were the same there as in all other places—at first very fair and friendly, tho' afterwards they gave great proofs of their deceitfulness. However, by the help of the Indian provisions the English chiefly subsisted till the return of the ships the next year, when two vessels were sent thither full freighted with men and provisions for supply of the plantation, one of which only arrived directly and the other being beat off to the Caribbean Islands did not arrive till the former was sailed hence again.

In the interval of these ships returning from England, the English had a very advantageous trade with the Indians and might have made much greater gains of it and managed it both to the greater satisfaction of the Indians and the greater ease and security of themselves if they had been under any rule or subject to any method in trade and not left at liberty to outvie or outbid one another; by which they not only cut short their own profit but created jealousies and disturbances among the Indians by letting one have a better bargain than another. For they being unaccustomed to barter, such of them as had been hardest dealt by in their commodities thought themselves cheated and abused, and so conceived a grudge against the English in general, making it a national quarrel. And this seems to be the original cause of most of their subsequent misfortunes by the Indians.

What also gave a greater interruption to this trade was an object that drew all their eyes and thoughts aside, even from taking the necessary care for their preservation and for support of their lives. Which was this: they found in a neck of land on the back of Jamestown Island a fresh stream of water springing out of a small bank which washed down with it a yellow sort of dust isinglass, which being cleansed by the fresh streaming of the water lay shining in the bottom of that limpid element and stirred up in them an unseasonable and inordinate desire after riches. For they, taking all to be gold that glistered, run into the utmost distraction, neglecting both the necessary defense of their lives from the Indians and the support of their bodies by securing of provisions; absolutely relying, like Midas, upon the almighty power of gold, thinking that where this was in plenty nothing could be wanting. But they soon grew sensible of their error and found that if this gilded dirt had been real gold, it could have been of no advantage to them. For by their negligence they were reduced to an exceeding scarcity of provisions, and that little they had was lost by the burning of their town while all hands were employed upon this imaginary golden treasure; so that they were forced to live for some time upon the wild fruits of the earth and upon crabs, mussels, and such like, not having a day's provision beforehand, as some of the laziest Indians who have no pleasure in exercise and won't be at the pains to fish and hunt. And, indeed, not so well as they neither, for by this careless neglecting of their defense against the Indians many of 'em were destroyed by that cruel people, and the rest durst not venture abroad but were forced to be content with what fell just into their mouths.

In this condition they were when the first ship of the two before mentioned came to their assistance; but their golden dreams overcame all difficulties. They spoke not nor thought of anything but gold, and that was all the lading that most of them were willing to take care for. Accordingly, they put into this ship all the yellow dirt they had gathered and what skins and furs they had trucked for, and filling her up with cedar, sent her away.

After she was gone, the other ship arrived, which they stowed likewise with this supposed gold dust, designing never to be poor again; filling her up with cedar and clapboard.

Those two ships being thus dispatched, they made several discoveries in James River and up Chesapeake Bay by the undertaking and management of Captain John Smith. And the year 1608 was the first year in which they gathered Indian corn of their own planting.

While these discoveries were making by Captain Smith, matters run again into confusion in Jamestown and several uneasy people, taking advantage of his absence, attempted to desert the settlement and run away with the small vessel that was left to attend upon it. For Captain Smith was the only man among them that could manage the discoveries with success, and he was the only man too that could keep the settlement in order. Thus the English continued to give themselves as much perplexity by their own distraction as the Indians did by their watchfulness and resentments.

3

Showing What Happened After the Alteration of the Government from an Elective President to a Commissionated Governor, Until the Dissolution of the Company

In the meanwhile the treasurer, Council, and Company of Virginia Adventurers in London, not finding that return and profit from the adventures they expected, and rightly judging that this disappointment as well as the idle quarrels in the colony proceeded from a mismanage of the government, petitioned his Majesty and got a new patent with leave to appoint a governor.

Upon this new grant they sent out nine ships and plentiful

supplies of men and provisions, and made three joint commissioners or governors in equal power, viz., Sir Thomas Gates, Sir George Somers, and Captain Newport. They agreed to go all together in one ship.

This ship, on board of which the three governors had embarked, being separated from the rest, was put to great distress in a severe storm, and after three days' and nights' constant bailing and pumping, was at last cast ashore at Bermuda and there staved; but by good providence the company was preserved.

Notwithstanding this shipwreck and extremity they were put to, yet could not this common misfortune make them agree. The best of it was they found plenty of provisions in that island and no Indians to annoy them. But still they quarrelled amongst themselves, and none more than the two knights, who made their parties, built each of them a cedar vessel, one called the *Patience* the other the *Deliverance*, and used what they gathered of the furniture of the old ship for rigging, and fish oil and hogs' grease mixed with lime and ashes instead of pitch and tar; for they found great plenty of Spanish hogs in this island which are supposed to have swam ashore from some wrecks and there afterwards increased.

While these things were acting in Bermuda, Captain Smith, being very much burnt by the accidental firing of some gunpowder as he was upon a discovery in his boat, was forced for his cure sake and the benefit of a surgeon to take his passage for England in a ship that was then upon the point of sailing.

Several of the nine ships that came out with the three governors arrived with many of the passengers; some of which in their humors would not submit to the government there, pretending the new commission destroyed the old one, that governors were appointed instead of a president, and that they themselves were to be of the Council, and so would assume an independent power, inspiring the people with disobedience. By which means they became frequently exposed in great parties to the cruelty of the Indians. All sorts of discipline were laid aside and their necessary defense neglected, so that the Indians taking advantage of those divisions formed a strategem to destroy them root and branch. And indeed they did cut many of 'em off by massacring whole companies at a time, so that all the out settlements were deserted and the people that were not destroyed took refuge in Jamestown, except the small settlement at Kiquotan, where they had built themselves a little fort and called it Algernon Fort. And yet, for all this, they continued their disorders, wasting their old provisions and neglecting to gather others, so that they who remained alive were all near famished, having brought themselves to that pass that they durst not stir from their own doors to gather the fruits of the earth or the crabs and mussels from the waterside, much less to hunt or catch wild beasts, fish, or fowl, which were found in great abundance there. They continued in these scanty circumstances till they were at last reduced to such extremity as to eat the very hides of their horses and the bodies of the Indians they had killed. And sometimes also upon a pinch they would not disdain to dig them up again to make a homely meal of after they had been buried. And that time is to this day remembered by the name of the Starving Time.

Thus a few months' indiscreet management brought such an infamy upon the country that to this day it cannot be wiped away. And the sicknesses occasioned by this bad diet, or rather want of diet, are unjustly remembered to the disadvantage of the country as a fault in the climate, which was only the foolishness and indiscretion of those who assumed the power of governing. I call it assumed because the new commission mentioned, by which they pretend to be of the Council, was not in all this time arrived but remained in Bermuda with the new governors.

Here I can't but admire the care, labor, courage, and understanding that Captain John Smith showed in the time of his administration; who not only founded but also preserved all these settlements in good order while he was amongst them. And without him they had certainly all been destroyed, either by famine or the enemy long before, tho' the country naturally afforded subsistence enough even without any other labor than that of gathering and preserving its spontaneous provisions.

For the first three years that Captain Smith was with them they never had in that whole time above six months' English provisions. But as soon as he had left 'em to themselves, all went to ruin, for the Indians had no longer any fear for themselves or friendship for the English. And six months after this gentleman's departure the five hundred men that he left were reduced to three score; and they, too, must of necessity have starved if their relief had been withheld a week longer.

In the meantime the three governors put to sea from Bermuda in their two small vessels with their company, to the number of 150, and in fourteen days, viz., the 25th of May, 1610, they arrived both together in Virginia and went with their vessels up to Jamestown, where they found the small remainder of the five hundred men in that melancholy way I just now hinted.

Sir Thomas Gates, Sir George Somers, and Captain Newport, the governors, were very compassionate of their condition and called a Council, wherein they informed them that they had but sixteen days' provision aboard, and therefore desired to know their opinion whether they would venture to sea under such a scarcity. Or if they resolved to continue in the settlement and take their fortunes, they would stay likewise and share the provisions among them, but desired that their determination might be speedy. They soon came to the conclusion of returning for England. But because their provisions were short, they resolved to go by the Banks of Newfoundland in hopes of meeting with some of the fishermen (this being now the season) and dividing themselves among their ships for the greater certainty of provision and for their better accommodation.

According to this resolution they all went aboard and fell down to Hog Island the 9th of June at night, and the next morning to Mulberry Island Point, which is eighteen miles below Jamestown and thirty above the mouth of the river. And there they spied a longboat which the Lord Delaware (who was just arrived with three ships) had sent before him up the river sounding the channel. His Lordship was made sole governor and was accompanied by several gentlemen of condition. He caused all the men to return again to Jamestown, resettled them with satisfaction and stayed with them till March following, and then being very sick he returned for England, leaving about two hundred in the colony.

On the 10th of May, 1611, Sir Thomas Dale, being then made governor, arrived with three ships which brought supplies of men, cattle, and hogs. He found them growing again into the like disorders as before, taking no care to plant corn and wholly relying upon their store, which then had but three months' provision in it. He therefore set them to work about corn, and tho' it was the middle of May before they began to prepare the ground, yet they had an indifferent good crop.

In August the same year Sir Thomas Gates arrived at Jamestown with six ships more and with a plentiful supply of hogs, cattle, fowls, etc., with a good quantity of ammunition and all other things necessary for a new colony, and besides this a reinforcement of 350 chosen men. In the beginning of September he settled a new town at Arrahattuck, about fifty miles above Jamestown, paling in the neck above two miles from the point from one reach of the river to the other. Here he built forts and sentry boxes, and in honor of Henry, Prince of Wales, called it Henrico. And also run a palissado on the other side of the river at Coxendale to secure their hogs.

Anno 1612: Two ships more arrived with supplies. And Captain Argall, who commanded one of them, being sent in her to Potomac to buy corn, he there met with Pocahontas, the excellent daughter of Powhatan. And having prevailed with her to come aboard to a treat, he detained her prisoner and carried her to Jamestown, designing to make peace with her father by her release. But on the contrary, that prince resented the affront very highly, and although he loved his daughter with all imaginable tenderness, yet he would not be brought to terms by that unhandsome treachery; till about two years after, a marriage being proposed between Mr. John Rolfe, an English gentleman, and this lady, which Powhatan taking to be a sincere token of friendship, he vouchsafed to consent to it and to conclude a peace.

Intermarriage had been indeed the method proposed very often by the Indians in the beginning, urging it frequently as a certain rule that the English were not their friends if they refused it. And I can't but think it would have been happy for that country had they embraced this proposal, for the jealousy of the Indians, which I take to be the cause of most of the rapines and murders they committed, would by this means have been altogether prevented and consequently the abundance of blood that was shed on both sides would have been saved. The great extremities they were so often reduced to by which so many died, would not have happened; the colony, instead of all these losses of men on both sides, would have been increasing in children to its advantage; the country would have escaped the odium which undeservedly fell upon it by the errors and convulsions in the first management; and, in all likelihood, many if not most of the Indians would have been converted to Christianity by this kind method; the country would have been full of people by the preservation of the many Christians and Indians that fell in the wars between them. Besides, there would have been a continuance of all those nations of Indians that are now dwindled away to nothing by their frequent removals or are fled to other parts, not to mention the invitation that so much success and prosperity would have been for others to have gone over and settled there instead of the frights and terrors that were produced by all those misfortunes that happened.

Pocahontas being thus married in the year 1613, a firm peace was concluded with her father, tho' he would not trust himself at her wedding. Both the English and Indians thought themselves entirely secure and quiet. This brought in the Chickahominy Indians also, tho' not out of any kindness or respect to the English, but out of fear of being by their assistance brought under Powhatan's absolute subjection, who used now and then to threaten and tyrannize over them.

Sir Thomas Dale returning for England, anno 1616, took with him Mr. Rolfe and his wife Pocahontas, who upon the marriage was christened and called Rebecca. He left Captain George Yeardley deputy governor during his absence, the country being then entirely at peace, and arrived at Plymouth the 12th of June.

Captain Yeardley made but a very ill governor. He let the buildings and forts go to ruin, not regarding the security of the people against the Indians, neglecting the corn, and applying all hands to plant tobacco, which promised the most immediate gain. In this condition they were when Captain Samuel Argall was sent thither governor, anno 1617, who found the number of people reduced to something more than four hundred, of which not above half were fit for labor. In the meanwhile the Indians mixing among 'em got experience daily in firearms, and some of 'em were instructed therein by the English themselves and employed to hunt and kill wild fowl for them, so great was their security upon this marriage. But Governor Argall, not liking those methods, regulated them on his arrival, and Captain Yeardley returned to England.

Governor Argall made the colony flourish and increase wonderfully and kept them in great plenty and quiet. The next year, viz., anno 1618, the Lord Delaware was sent over again with two hundred men more for the settlement, with other necessaries suitable. But sailing by the Western Islands they met with contrary winds and great sickness, so that about thirty of them died, among which the Lord Delaware was one. By which means the government there still continued in the hands of Captain Argall.

Powhatan died in April the same year, leaving his second brother Itopatin in possession of his empire, a prince far short of the parts of Opechancanough, who by some was said to be his elder brother, and then king of Chickahominy, but he having debauched them from the allegiance of Powhatan was disinherited by him. This Opechancanough was a cunning and a brave prince who soon grasped all the empire to himself. But at first they jointly renewed the peace with the English upon the accession of Itopatin to the crown.

[In 1619] And soon after Captain Yeardley being knighted was sent governor thither again. Very great supplies of cattle and other provisions were sent there that year, and likewise a thousand or twelve hundred men. They resettled all their old plantations that had been deserted, made additions to the number of the Council, and called an assembly of burgesses from all parts of the country, which were to be elected by the people in their several plantations.

These burgesses met the governor and Council at Jamestown in August, 1619, and sat in consultation in the same house with them, as the method of the Scots' Parliament is, debating matters for the improvement and good government of the country.

This was the first General Assembly that ever was held there. I heartily wish, tho' they did not unite their houses again, they would, however, unite their endeavors and affections for the good of the country.

In August [also] a Dutch man-of-war landed twenty Negroes for sale which were the first of that kind that were carried into the country.

Thus Virginia continued to flourish and increase, great supplies continually arriving, and new settlements being made all over the country. A salt work was set up at Cape Charles on the Eastern Shore, and an iron work at Falling Creek in James River, where they made proof of good iron ore and brought the whole work so near perfection that they writ word to the Company in London that they did not doubt but to finish the work and have plentiful provision of iron for them by the next Easter. At that time the fame of the plenty and riches in which the English lived there was very great, and Sir George Yeardley now had all the appearance of making amends for the errors of his former government. Nevertheless, he let them run into the same sleepiness and security as before, neglecting all thoughts of a necessary defense, which laid the foundation of the following calamities.

It was October, 1621, that Sir Francis Wyatt arrived governor, and in November Captain Newport arrived with fifty men imported at his own charge, besides passengers, and made a plantation at Newport's News, naming it after himself. The governor made a review of all the settlements and suffered new ones to be made even as far as the Potomac River. This ought to be observed of the Eastern Shore Indians—that they never gave the English any trouble, but courted and befriended them from first to last. Perhaps the English by the time they came to settle those parts had considered how to rectify their former mismanagement and learned better methods of regulating their trade with the Indians and of treating them more kindly than at first.

In the meantime, by the great increase of people and the long quiet they had enjoyed among the Indians since the marriage of Pocahontas and the accession of Opechancanough to the imperial crown, all men were lulled into a fatal security and became everywhere familiar with the Indians—eating, drinking, and sleeping amongst them, by which means they became perfectly acquainted with all our English strength and the use of our arms, knowing at all times when and where to find our people, whether at home or in the woods, in bodies or dispersed, in condition of defense or indefensible. This exposing of their weakness gave them occasion to think more contemptibly of them than otherwise, perhaps, they would have done, for which reason they became more peevish and more hardy to attempt anything against them.

Thus upon the loss of one of their leading men (a war captain, as they call him) who was likewise supposed to be justly killed, Opechancanough took affront and in revenge laid the plot of a general massacre of the English to be executed on the 22d of

March, 1622, a little before noon, at a time when our men were all at work abroad in their plantations, dispersed and unarmed. This hellish contrivance was to take effect upon all the several settlements at one and the same instant except on the Eastern Shore, whither this plot did not reach. The Indians had been made so familiar with the English as to borrow their boats and canoes to cross the rivers in, when they went to consult with their neighboring Indians upon this execrable conspiracy. And, to color their design the better, they brought presents of deer, turkeys, fish, and fruits to the English the evening before. The very morning of the massacre they came freely and unarmed among them, eating with them and behaving themselves with the same freedom and friendship as formerly till the very minute they were to put their plot in execution. Then they fell to work all at once everywhere, knocking the English unawares on the head, some with their hatchets, which they call tomahawks, others with the hoes and axes of the English themselves, shooting at those who escaped the reach of their hands, sparing neither age nor sex but destroying man, woman, and child according to their cruel way of leaving none behind to bear resentment. But whatever was not done by surprise that day was left undone, and many that made early resistance escaped.

By the account taken of the Christians murdered that morning, they were found to be 347, most of them falling by their own instruments and working tools.

This gave the English a fair pretense of endeavoring the total extirpation of the Indians, but more especially of Opechancanough and his nation. Accordingly, they set themselves about it, making use of the Roman maxim (Faith is not to be kept with heretics) to obtain their ends. For after some months' fruitless pursuit of them, who could too dexterously hide themselves in the woods, the English pretended articles of peace, giving them all manner of fair words and promises of oblivion. They designed thereby (as their own letters now on record and their own actions thereupon prove) to draw the Indians back and entice them to plant their corn on their habitations nearest adjoining to the English, and then to cut it up when the summer should be too far spent to leave them hopes of another crop that year, by which means they proposed to bring them to want necessaries and starve. And the

English did so far accomplish their ends as to bring the Indians to plant their corn at their usual habitations, whereby they gained an opportunity of repaying them some part of the debt in their own coin, for they fell suddenly upon them, cut to pieces such of them as could not make their escape, and afterwards totally destroyed their corn.

Another effect of the massacre of the English was the reducing all their settlements again to six or seven in number for their better defense. Besides, it was such a disheartening to some good projects then just advancing that to this day they have never been put in execution, namely, the glass houses in Jamestown and the iron work at Falling Creek, which has been already mentioned. The massacre fell so hard upon this last place that no soul was saved but a boy and a girl who with great difficulty hid themselves.

The superintendent of this iron work had also discovered a vein of lead ore which he kept private and made use of it to furnish all the neighbors with bullets and shot. But he being cut off with the rest and the secret not having been communicated, this lead mine could never after be found till Colonel Byrd some few years ago prevailed with an Indian under pretense of hunting to give him a sign by dropping his tomahawk at the place (he not daringly publicly to discover it for fear of being murdered). The sign was accordingly given and the company at that time found several pieces of good lead ore upon the surface of the ground and marked the trees thereabouts. Notwithstanding which, I know not by what witchcraft it happens, but no mortal to this day could ever find that place again, tho' it be upon part of the colonel's own possessions. And so it rests till time and thicker settlements discover it.

Thus the Company of Adventurers having by those frequent acts of mismanagement met with vast losses and misfortunes, many grew sick of it and parted with their shares, and others came into their places and promoted the sending in fresh recruits of men and goods. But the chief design of all parties concerned was to fetch away the treasure from thence, aiming more at sudden gain than to form any regular colony or establish a settlement in such a manner as to make it a lasting happiness to the country.

Several gentlemen went over upon their particular stocks, sep-

arate from that of the Company, with their own servants and
goods, each designing to obtain land from the government as
Captain Newport had done; or at least to obtain patents according to the regulation for granting lands to Adventurers. Others
sought their grants of the Company in London and obtained
authorities and jurisdiction as well as land distinct from the
authority of the government, which was the foundation of great
disorder and the occasion of their following misfortunes. Among
others, one Captain Martin, having made very considerable preparations towards a settlement, obtained a suitable grant of land
and was made of the Council there. But he, grasping still at more,
hankered after dominion as well as possession and caused so
many differences that at last he put all things into distraction;
insomuch that the Indians, still seeking revenge, took advantage
of these dissensions and fell foul again of the English, gratifying
their vengeance with new bloodshed.

The fatal consequences of the Company's maladministration
cried so loud that King Charles the First, coming to the Crown of
England, had a tender concern for the poor people that had been
betrayed thither and lost. Upon which consideration he dissolved
the Company in the year 1624, reducing the country and government into his own immediate direction, appointing the governor
and Council himself, and ordering all patents and process to issue
in his own name, reserving only to himself an easy quitrent of two
shillings for every hundred acres, and so *pro rato*.

4

Containing the History of the Government
from the Dissolution of the Company
to the Year 1704

The country being thus taken into the king's hands, his Majesty
was pleased to establish the constitution to be by a governor,
Council, and Assembly. He likewise confirmed the rules and orders
made by the first Assembly for apportioning the land and granting patents to particular adventurers.

This was a constitution according to their hearts' desire, and things seemed now to go on in a happy course for encouragement of the colony. People flocked over thither apace. Everyone took up land by patent to his liking, and, not minding anything but to be masters of great tracts of land, they planted themselves separately on their several plantations. Nor did they fear the Indians, but kept them at a greater distance than formerly; and they for their parts, seeing the English so sensibly increase in number, were glad to keep their distance and be peaceable.

This liberty of taking up land and the ambition each man had of being lord of a vast tho' unimproved territory, together with the advantage of the many rivers which afforded a commodious road for shipping at every man's door, has made the country fall into such an unhappy settlement and course of trade that to this day they have not any one place of cohabitation among them that may reasonably bear the name of a town.

The constitution being thus firmly established and continuing its course regularly for some time, people began to lay aside all fears of any future misfortune. Several gentlemen of condition went over with their whole families, some for bettering their estates, others for religion and other reasons best known to themselves. Among those, that noble Cecilius Calvert, Lord Baltimore, a Roman Catholic, thought for the more quiet exercise of his religion to retire with his family into that New World.

By this unhappy accident a country which nature had so well contrived for one became two separate governments. This produced a most unhappy inconvenience to both. For these two being the only countries under the dominion of England that plant tobacco in any quantity, the consequence of that division is that when one colony goes about to prohibit the trash of that commodity to help the market, then the other, to take advantage of that market, pours into England all they can make, both good and bad, without distinction. This is very injurious to the other colony, which had voluntarily suffered so great a diminution in the quantity to mend the quality.

Neither was this all the mischief that happened to poor Virginia upon this grant, for the example of it had dreadful consequences and was in the end one of the occasions of another massacre by the Indians. For this precedent of my Lord Baltimore's grant, which entrenched upon the charters and bounds of Virginia, was hint enough for other courtiers (who never intended settlement as my lord did) to find out something of the same kind to make money of. This was the occasion of several very large defalcations from Virginia within a few years afterwards which were forwarded and assisted by the contrivance of the governor, Sir John Harvey. Insomuch that not only the land itself, quitrents and all, but the authorities and jurisdictions that belonged to that colony were given away; nay, sometimes in those unjust grants he included the very settlements that had been before made, countenancing them with the usual pretense of his Majesty's instructions.

As this gentleman was irregular in this, so he was very unjust and arbitrary in his other methods of government. He improved the fines and penalties which the unwary Assemblies of those times had given chiefly to himself. He was so haughty and furious to the Council and to the best gentlemen of the country that his tyranny grew at last unsupportable, so that in the year 1639 the Council sent him a prisoner to London, and with him two of their number to maintain the articles against him. This news being brought to King Charles I, his Majesty was very much displeased, and without hearing anything caused him to return [the] governor again. But by the next shipping he was graciously pleased to change him, and so made amends for this man's maladministration by sending [in 1642] the good and just Sir William Berkeley to succeed him.

While these things were transacting, there was so general a dissatisfaction occasioned by the oppressions of Sir John Harvey and the difficulties in getting him out that the whole colony was in confusion. The subtle Indians, who took all advantages, resented the encroachments upon them by his grants. They see the English uneasy and disunited among themselves, and by the direction of Opechancanough, their king, laid the groundwork of another massacre [in 1644], wherein by surprise they cut off near five hundred Christians more. But this execution did not take so general effect as formerly, because the Indians were not so frequently suffered to come among the inner habitations of the English. And therefore the massacre fell severest on the south side of James River and on the heads of the other rivers, but chiefly of York River where the emperor Opechancanough kept the seat of his government.

This Opechancanough was a man of large stature, noble presence, and extraordinary parts. Tho' he had no advantage of literature (that being nowhere to be found among the Indians), yet he was perfectly skilled in the art of governing his rude countrymen. He caused all the Indians far and near to dread his name and had them all entirely in subjection.

This king in Smith's *History* is called brother to Powhatan, but by the Indians he was not so esteemed. For they say he was a prince of a foreign nation and came to them a great way from the southwest. And by their accounts we suppose him to have come from the Spanish Indians somewhere near Mexico or the mines of St. Barbe. But be that matter how it will, from that time till his captivity there never was the least truce between them and the English.

Sir William Berkeley upon his arrival showed such an opposition to the unjust grants made by Sir John Harvey that very few of them took effect; and such as did were subjected to the settled conditions of the other parts of the government and made liable to the payment of the full quitrents. He encouraged the country in several essays of potash, soap, salt, flax, hemp, silk, and cotton. But the Indian war, ensuing upon Opechancanough's massacre, was a great obstruction to these good designs by requiring all the spare men to be employed in defense of the country.

Opechancanough, by his great age and the fatigues of war (in which Sir William Berkeley followed him close), was now grown so decrepit that he was not able to walk alone, but was carried about by his men wherever he had a mind to move. His flesh was all macerated, his sinews slackened, and his eyelids became so heavy that he could not see but as they were lifted up by his servants. In this low condition he was when Sir William Berkeley, hearing that he was at some distance from his usual habitation, resolved at all adventures to seize his person, which he happily effected. For with a party of horse he made a speedy march, surprised him in his quarters, and brought him prisoner to Jamestown, where by the governor's command he was treated with all the respect and tenderness imaginable. Sir William had a mind to send him to England, hoping to get reputation by presenting his Majesty with a royal captive who at his pleasure could call into the field ten times more Indians than Sir William Berkeley had

English in his whole government. Besides, he thought this ancient prince would be an instance of the healthiness and long life of the natives of that country. However, he could not preserve his life above a fortnight, for one of the soldiers, resenting the calamities the colony had suffered by this prince's means, basely shot him thro' the back after he was made prisoner; of which wound he died.

He continued brave to the last moment of his life and showed not the least dejection at his captivity. He heard one day a great noise of the treading of people about him, upon which he caused his eyelids to be lifted up and finding that a crowd of people were let in to see him he called in high indignation for the governor; who being come, Opechancanough scornfully told him that had it been his fortune to take Sir William Berkeley prisoner he should not meanly have exposed him as a show to the people.

After this Sir William Berkeley made a new peace with the Indians which continued for a long time unviolated; insomuch that all the thoughts of future injury from them were laid aside. But he himself did not long enjoy the benefit of this profound peace, for the unhappy troubles of King Charles I increasing in England proved a great disturbance to him and to all the people. They, to prevent the infection from reaching that country, made severe laws against the Puritans, tho' there were as yet none among them. But all correspondence with England was interrupted, the supplies lessened, and trade obstructed. In a word, all people were impatient to know what would be the event of so much confusion.

At last the king was traitorously beheaded in England and Oliver installed protector. However, his authority was not acknowledged in Virginia for several years after, till they were forced to it by the last necessity. For in the year 1651, by Cromwell's command, Captain Dennis with a squadron of men-of-war arrived there from the Caribbean Islands, where they had been subduing Barbados. The country at first held out vigorously against him, and Sir William Berkeley by the assistance of such Dutch vessels as were then there made a brave resistance. But at last Dennis contrived a stratagem which betrayed the country. He had got a considerable parcel of goods aboard which belonged to two of the Council, and found a method of informing them of it. By this means they were reduced to the dilemma either of submitting or losing their goods. This occasioned factions among them, so that at last, after the surrender of all the other English plantations, Sir William was forced to submit to the usurper on the terms of a general pardon. However, it ought to be remembered to his praise and to the immortal honor of that colony that it was the last of all the king's dominions that submitted to the usurpation and afterwards the first that cast it off.

Oliver had no sooner subdued the plantations but he began to contrive how to keep them under, so that they might never be able for the time to come to give him further trouble. To this end he thought it necessary to break off their correspondence with all other nations, thereby to prevent their being furnished with arms, ammunition, and other warlike provisions. According to this design he contrived a severe act of Parliament, whereby he prohibited the plantations from receiving or exporting any European commodities but what should be carried to them by Englishmen and in English-built ships. They were absolutely forbid corresponding with any nation or colony not subject to the Crown of England. Neither was any alien suffered to manage a trade or factory in any of them. In all which things the plantations had been till then indulged, for their encouragement.

Notwithstanding this Act of Navigation [of 1651], the protector never thought the plantations enough secured, but frequently changed their governors to prevent their intriguing with the people. So that during the small time of his protectorship they had no less than three governors there—namely, Digges, Bennett, and Mathews.

The strange arbitrary curbs he put upon the plantations exceedingly afflicted the people. He had the inhumanity to forbid them all manner of trade and correspondence with other nations at a time when England itself was in distraction and could neither take off their commodities nor supply them sufficiently with its own. Neither had they ever been used to supply them with half the commodities they expended or to take off above half the tobacco they made. Such violent proceedings made the people desperate and inspired them with a desire to use the last remedy to relieve themselves from his lawless usurpation. In a short time afterwards a fair opportunity happened, for Governor Mathews died and no person was substituted to succeed him in the government. Whereupon the people applied themselves to Sir William Berkeley (who had continued all this time upon his own plantation in a private capacity) and unanimously chose him their governor again.

Sir William Berkeley had all along retained an unshaken loyalty for the royal family, and therefore generously told the people that he could not approve of the protector's oppression and was resolved never to serve anybody but the lawful heir to the Crown; and that if he accepted the government it should be upon their solemn promise after his example to venture their lives and fortunes for the king, who was then in France.

This was their dearest wish, and therefore with a unanimous voice they told him that they were ready to hazard all for the king. Now, this was actually before the king's return for England, and proceeded from a brave principle of loyalty for which they had no example. Sir William Berkeley embraced their choice and forthwith proclaimed Charles II king of England, Scotland, France, Ireland, and Virginia, and caused all process to be issued in his name. Thus his Majesty was actually king in Virginia before he was so in England. But it pleased God to restore him soon after to the throne of his ancestors, and so that country escaped being chastised for throwing off the usurpation.

Upon the king's restoration, he sent Sir William Berkeley a new commission with leave to return to England and power to appoint a deputy in his absence. For his Majesty in his exile had received intelligence of this gentleman's loyalty and during that time had renewed his commission.

Upon this Sir William Berkeley appointed Colonel Francis Moryson deputy governor and went for England to wait on his Majesty, by whom he was kindly received. At his return he carried his Majesty's pressing instructions for encouraging the people in husbandry and manufactures, but more especially to promote silk and vineyards. There is a tradition that the king in compliment to that colony wore at his coronation a robe made of the silk that was sent from thence. But this was all the reward the country had for their loyalty, for the Parliament was pleased to renew the act contrived by the usurper for discouraging the plantations with severer restraints and prohibitions by bonds, securities, etc.

During the time of Sir William Berkeley's absence, Colonel

Moryson had, according to his directions, revised the laws and compiled them into one body, ready to be confirmed by the Assembly at his return. By these laws the Church of England was confirmed the established religion, the charge of the government sustained, trade and manufactures were encouraged, a town projected, and all the Indian affairs settled.

The parishes were likewise regulated, competent allowances were made to the ministers to the value of about fourscore pounds a year besides glebes and perquisites, and the method of their preferment was settled. Convenient churches and glebes were provided and all necessary parish officers instituted. Some steps were made also towards a free school and college, and all the poor effectually provided for.

For support of the government the duty of two shillings per hogshead on all tobacco, and that of one shilling per ton fort duty on shipping, were made perpetual; and the collectors were obliged to account for the same to the General Assembly.

For encouragement of manufactures, prizes were appointed for the makers of the best pieces of linen and woolen cloth, and a reward of fifty pounds of tobacco was given for each pound of silk. All persons were enjoined to plant mulberry trees for the food of the silkworm according to the number of acres of land they held. Tanhouses were set up in each county at the county charge, and public encouragement was given to a salt work on the Eastern Shore. A reward was appointed in proportion to the tonnage of all sea vessels built there, and an exemption allowed from all fees and duties payable by such shipping.

Peace and commerce with the Indians was settled by law and their boundaries prescribed. Several other good acts were made suiting the necessity of the government, so that nothing then seemed to remain but the improvement of the country and encouragement of those manufactures the king had been pleased to recommend, together with such others as should be found beneficial.

Sir William Berkeley, being then again in full possession of his government and at perfect peace with the Indians, set all hands industriously to work in making country improvements. He passed a new act for encouragement of Jamestown, whereby several houses were built therein at the charge of several counties. However, the main ingredient for the advancement of towns was still wanting—namely, the confinement of all shipping and trade to them only; by defect of which all the other expedients availed nothing, for most of the buildings were soon converted into houses of entertainment.

Anno 1663: divers sectaries in religion beginning to spread themselves there, by a mistaken zeal great restraints were laid upon them under severe penalties to prevent their increase.

This made many of them fly to other colonies and prevented abundance of others from going over to seat themselves among 'em. And as the former ill treatment of my Lord Baltimore kept many people away and drove others to Maryland, so the present severities towards the Nonconformists robbed them of many more who went to the neighboring colonies and might otherwise have contributed vastly to the improvement of that.

The rigorous circumspection of their trade, the persecution of their sectaries, and the little demand of tobacco had like to have had very fatal consequences. For the poor people becoming thereby very uneasy, their murmurings were watched and fed by several mutinous and rebellious Oliverian soldiers that were sent thither as servants. These, depending upon the discontented people of all sorts, formed a villainous plot to destroy their masters and afterwards to set up for themselves.

This plot was brought so near to perfection that it was the very night before the designed execution ere it was discovered, and then it came out by the relenting of one of their accomplices, whose name was Birkenhead. This man was servant to Mr. Smith of Purton in Gloucester County, near which place, viz., at Poplar Spring, the miscreants were to meet the night following and put in execution their horrid conspiracy.

Upon this discovery by Birkenhead, notice was immediately sent to the governor at Green Spring. And the method he took to prevent it was by private orders that some of the militia should meet before the time at the place where the conspirators were to rendezvous and seize them as they came singly up to it. Which orders being happily executed, their devilish plot was defeated. However, there were but a few taken, because several of them making their escape turned back such of their fellows as they met on the road and prevented most of them from coming up or from being discovered.

Four of these rogues were hanged, but Birkenhead was gratified with his freedom and a reward of two hundred pounds sterling.

For the discovery and happy disappointment of this plot, an anniversary thanksgiving was appointed on the 13th of September, the day it was to have been put in execution. And it is great pity some other days are not commemorated as well as that.

The news of this plot being transmitted to King Charles II, his Majesty sent his royal commands to build a fort at Jamestown for security of the governor and to be a curb upon all such traitorous attempts for the future. But the country, thinking the danger over, only raised a battery of some small pieces of cannon.

Another misfortune happened to the plantation this year, which was a new [Navigation] Act of Parliament in England, laying a severer restraint upon their supplies than formerly. By this act they could have no foreign goods which were not first landed in England and carried directly from thence to the plantations, the former restraint of importing them only by Englishmen in English-built shipping not being thought sufficient.

This was a misfortune that cut with a double edge; for, first, it reduced their staple tobacco to a very low price; and, secondly, it raised the value of European goods to what the merchants pleased to put upon them.

For this their Assembly could think of no remedy but to be even with the merchants and make their tobacco scarce by prohibiting the planting of it for one year, and during that idle year to invite the people to enter upon manufactures. But Maryland not concurring in this project, they were obliged in their own defense to repeal the act of Assembly again and return to their old drudgery of planting tobacco.

The country thus missed of their remedy in the stint of tobacco, which, on the contrary, multiplied exceedingly by the great increase of servants. This, together with the above mentioned curbs on trade, exasperated the people, because now they found themselves under a necessity of exchanging their commodities with the merchants of England at their own terms. The Assembly therefore again attempted the stint of tobacco and passed another act against planting it for one year. And Carolina and Maryland both agreed to it. But some accident hindering the agent of Carolina from giving notice thereof to Maryland by the day appointed, the governor of that province proclaimed the act void, altho' everybody there knew that Carolina had fully agreed to all things required of them. But he took advantage of this nice punctilio, because of the loss such a diminution would have been to his annual income, and so all people relapsed again into the disease of planting tobacco.

Virginia was more nettled at this ill usage from Maryland than at her former absolute denial. But being conscious of their own low condition, they were resolved to take all patiently and by fair means get relief if they could. They therefore appointed agents to reassume the treaty and submitted so low as to send them to St. Marys, then the residence of the governor of Maryland and the place where the Assemblies met. Yet all this condescension could not hold them to their bargain. The governor said he had observed his part of the agreement and would not call an Assembly any more upon that subject.

In this manner two whole years were spent, and nothing could be accomplished for their relief. In the meanwhile England was studious to prevent their receiving supplies from any other country. To do that more effectually it was thought expedient to confine the trade of that colony to one place, but that not being found practicable because of the many great rivers that divide their habitations and the extraordinary conveniences of each, his Majesty sent directions to build forts in the several rivers and enjoined all the ships to ride under those forts, and further ordered that those places only should be the ports of trade.

This instruction was punctually observed for a year, and preparations were made for ports by casting up breastworks in such places as the Assembly appointed; and shipping did for that time ride at those places. But the great fire and plague happening in London immediately upon it made their supplies that year very uncertain, and the terror the people were in lest the plague should be brought over with the goods from London prevented them from residing at those ports for fear of being all swept away at once. And so everybody was left at liberty again.

Still no favor could be obtained for the tobacco trade, and the English merchants afforded a bare sufficiency of clothing for their crops. The Assembly were full enough of resentment but overlooked their right way of redress. All they could do was to cause looms and workhouses to be set up in the several counties at the county charge. They renewed the rewards of silk and put great penalties upon every neglect of making flax and hemp. About this time they sustained some damage by the Dutch war, for which reason they ordered the forts to be rebuilt of brick; but having yet no true notion of the advantage of towns, they did not oblige the ships to ride under them, which thing alone well executed would have answered all their desires.

Sir William Berkeley, who was always contriving and industrious for the good of the country, was not contented to set a useful example at home by the essays he made of potash, flax, hemp, silk, etc., but was also resolved to make new discoveries abroad amongst the Indians.

For this end he employed a small company of about fourteen English and as many Indians, under the command of Captain Henry Batts, to go upon such an adventure. They set out together from Appomattox and in seven days' march reached the foot of the mountains. The mountains they first arrived at were not extraordinary high or steep, but after they had passed the first ridge they encountered others that seemed to reach the clouds and were so perpendicular and full of precipices that sometimes in a whole day's march they could not travel three miles in a direct line. In other places they found large level plains and fine savannas three or four miles wide, in which were an infinite quantity of turkeys, deer, elks, and buffaloes so gentle and undisturbed that they had no fear at the appearance of the men, but would suffer them to come almost within reach of their hands. There they also found grapes so prodigiously large that they seemed more like bullace [damson] than grapes. When they traversed these mountains, they came to a fine level country again and discovered a rivulet that descended backwards. Down that stream they traveled several days till they came to old fields and cabins where the Indians had lately been but were supposed to have fled at the approach of Batts and his company. However, the captain followed the old rule of leaving some toys in their cabins for them to find at their return, by which they might know they were friends. Near to these cabins were great marshes where the Indians which Captain Batts had with him made a halt and would positively proceed no further. They said that not far off from that place lived a nation of Indians that made

salt and sold it to their neighbors; that this was a great and powerful people which never suffered any strangers to return that had
once discovered their towns. Captain Batts used all the arguments
he could to get them forward, but in vain. And so, to please those
timorous Indians, the hopes of this discovery were frustrated and
the detachment was forced to return.

Upon Captain Batts' report to Sir William Berkeley, he resolved
to make a journey himself, that so there might be no hindrance for
want of sufficient authority as had been in the aforesaid expedition. To this end he concerted matters for it and had pitched upon
his deputy governor. The Assembly also made an act to encourage
it, but all these preparations came to nothing by the confusion
which happened there soon after by Bacon's Rebellion. And since
that there has never been any such discovery attempted from
Virginia.

The occasion of this rebellion is not easy to be discovered, but
'tis certain there were many things that concurred towards it.
For it cannot be imagined that upon the instigation of two or
three traders only who aimed at a monopoly of the Indian trade,
as some pretend to say, the whole country would have fallen into
so much distraction, in which people did not only hazard their
necks by rebellion but endeavored to ruin a governor whom they
all entirely loved and had unanimously chosen—a gentleman who
had devoted his whole life and estate to the service of the country
and against whom in thirty-five years' experience there had never
been one single complaint. Neither can it be supposed that upon so
slight grounds they would make choice of a leader they hardly
knew to oppose a gentleman that had been so long and so de-
servedly the darling of the people. So that in all probability there
was something else in the wind, without which the body of the
country had never been engaged in that insurrection.

Four things may be reckoned to have been the main ingredients
towards this intestine commotion, viz., first, the extreme low price
of tobacco and the ill usage of the planters in the exchange of
goods for it, which the country with all their earnest endeavors
could not remedy; secondly, the splitting the colony into proprieties, contrary to the original charters, and the extravagant taxes
they were forced to undergo to relieve themselves from those
grants; thirdly, the heavy restraints and burdens laid upon their

trade by act of Parliament in England; fourthly, the disturbance given by the Indians. Of all which I beg leave to speak in their order.

First, of the low price of tobacco and the disappointment of all sort of remedy I have spoken sufficiently before. Secondly, of splitting the country into proprieties.

King Charles II to gratify some nobles about him made two great grants out of that country. These grants were not of the uncultivated woodland only, but also of plantations which for many years had been seated and improved under the encouragement of several charters granted by his royal ancestors to that colony. Those grants were distinguished by the names of the Northern and Southern Grants of Virginia, and the same men were concerned in both. They were kept dormant some years after they were made, and in the year 1674 begun to be put in execution. As soon as ever the country came to know this, they remonstrated against them, and the Assembly drew up an humble address to his Majesty complaining of the said grant as derogatory to the previous charters and privileges granted to that colony by his Majesty and his royal progenitors. They sent to England Mr. Secretary Ludwell and Colonel Park as their agents to address the king to vacate those grants. And the better to defray that charge they laid a tax of fifty pounds of tobacco per poll for two years together, over and above all other taxes, which was an excessive burden. They likewise laid amercements of seventy, fifty, and thirty pounds of tobacco on every cause tried throughout the country. Besides all this they applied the balance remaining due upon account of the two shilling per hogshead and fort duties to this use. Which taxes and amercements fell heaviest on the poor people, the effect of whose labor would not clothe their wives and children. This made them desperately uneasy, especially when, after a whole year's patience under all these pressures, they had no encouragement from their agents in England to hope for remedy, nor any certainty when they should be eased of those heavy impositions.

Thirdly, upon the back of all these misfortunes came out the act of *25 Car. II* [1673] for better securing the plantation trade. By this act several duties were laid on the trade from one plantation to another. This was a new hardship and the rather because the revenue arising by this act was not applied to the use of the plantation wherein it was raised but given clear away. Nay, in that country it seemed to be of no other use but to create a good income to the officers, for the collector had half, the comptroller a quarter, and the remaining quarter was sub-divided into salaries till it was lost.

By the same act also very great duties were laid on the fisheries of the plantations, if manufactured by the English inhabitants there, while the people of England were absolutely free from all customs. Nay, tho' the oil, blubber, and whalebone which were made by the inhabitants of the plantations were carried to England by Englishmen and in English-built ships, yet it was held to a considerable duty.

These were the afflictions that country labored under when the fourth accident happened, viz., the disturbance offered by the Indians to the frontiers.

This was occasioned, first, by the Indians on the head of the Bay; secondly, by the Indians on their own frontiers.

First, the Indians at the head of the Bay drove a constant trade with the Dutch in Monadas, now called New York, and to carry on this they used to come and return every year by their frontiers of Virginia to purchase skins and furs of the Indians to the southward. This trade was carried on peaceably while the Dutch held Monadas, and the Indians used to call on the English to whom they would sell part of their furs and with the rest go on to Monadas. But after the English came to possess that place and understood the advantages the Virginians made by the trade of the Indians, they inspired them with such a hatred to the inhabitants of Virginia that instead of coming peaceably to trade with them, as they had done for several years before, they afterwards never came but only to commit robberies and murders upon the people.

Secondly, the Indians upon their own frontiers were likewise inspired with ill thoughts of 'em. For their Indian merchants had lost a considerable branch of their trade they knew not how, and apprehended the consequences of Sir William Berkeley's intended discoveries, which were espoused by the Assembly, might take away the remaining part of their profit. This made them very troublesome to the neighbor Indians, who on their part, observing an unusual uneasiness in the English and being terrified by their rough usage, immediately suspected some wicked design against their lives, and so fled to their remoter habitations. This confirmed the English in the belief that they had been the murderers, till at last they provoked them to be so in earnest.

This addition of mischief to minds already full of discontent made people ready to vent all their resentment against the poor Indians. There was nothing to be got by tobacco; neither could they turn any other manufacture to advantage, so that most of the poorer sort were willing to quit their unprofitable employments and go volunteers against the Indians.

At first they flocked together tumultuously, running in troops from one plantation to another without a head, till at last the seditious humor of Colonel Nathaniel Bacon led him to be of the party. This gentleman had been brought up at one of the Inns of Court in England and had a moderate fortune. He was young, bold, active, of an inviting aspect and powerful elocution—in a word, he was every way qualified to head a giddy and unthinking multitude. Before he had been three years in the country he was, for his extraordinary qualifications, made one of the Council, and in great honor and esteem among the people. For this reason he no sooner gave countenance to this riotous mob, but they all presently fixed their eyes upon him for their general and accordingly made their addresses to him. As soon as he found this, he harangued them publicly. He aggravated the Indian mischiefs, complaining that they were occasioned for want of a due regulation of their trade. He recounted particularly the other grievances and pressures they lay under and pretended that he accepted of their command with no other intention but to do them and the country service, in which he was willing to encounter the greater difficulties and dangers. He further assured them he would never lay down his arms till he had revenged their sufferings upon the Indians and redressed all their other grievances.

By these insinuations he wrought his men into so perfect a unanimity that they were one and all at his devotion. He took care to exasperate them to the utmost by representing all their misfortunes. After he had begun to muster them, he dispatched a messenger to the governor, by whom he aggravated the mischiefs done by the Indians and desired a commission of general to go out against them. This gentleman was in so great esteem at that time with the Council that the governor did not think fit to give him a flat refusal, but sent him word he would consult the Council and return him a further answer.

In the meantime, Bacon was expeditious in his preparation and, having all things in readiness, began his march, depending on the authority the people had given him. He would not lose so much time as to stay for his commission, but dispatched several messengers to the governor to hasten it. On the other hand, the governor instead of a commission sent positive orders to him to disperse his men and come down in person to him upon pain of being declared a rebel.

The unexpected order was a great surprise to Bacon and not a little trouble to his men. However, he was resolved to prosecute his first intentions, depending upon his strength and interest with the people. Nevertheless, he intended to wait upon the governor, but not altogether defenseless. Pursuant to this resolution, he took about forty of his men down with him in a sloop to Jamestown, where the governor was with his Council.

Matters did not succeed there to Mr. Bacon's satisfaction; wherefore he expressed himself a little too freely. For which being suspended from the Council, he went away again in a huff with his sloop and followers. The governor filled a longboat with men and pursued the sloop so close that Colonel Bacon removed into his boat to make more haste. But the governor had sent up by land to the ships at Sandy Point, where he was stopped and sent down again. Upon his return he was kindly received by the governor, who, knowing he had gone a step beyond his instructions in having suspended him, was glad to admit him again of the Council, after which he hoped all things might be pacified.

Notwithstanding this, Colonel Bacon still insisted upon a commission to be general of the volunteers and to go out against the Indians; from which the governor endeavored to dissuade him, but to no purpose, because he had some secret project in view. He had the luck to be countenanced in his importunities by the news of fresh murder and robberies committed by the Indians. However, not being able to accomplish his ends by fair means, he stole privately out of town, and, having put himself at the head of six hundred volunteers, marched directly to Jamestown, where the Assembly was then sitting. He presented himself before the

Assembly and drew up his men in battalia before the house wherein they sat. He urged to them his preparations and alleged that if the commission had not been delayed so long the war against the Indians might have been finished.

The governor resented this insolent usage worst of all, and now obstinately refused to grant him anything, offering his naked breast against the presented arms of his followers. But the Assembly, fearing the fatal consequence of provoking a discontented multitude ready armed who had the governor, Council, and Assembly entirely in their power, addressed the governor to grant Bacon his request. They prepared themselves the commission, constituting him general of the forces of Virginia, and brought it to the governor to be signed.

With much reluctancy his Excellency signed it, and thereby put the power of war and peace into Bacon's hands. Upon this he marched away immediately, having gained his end, which was in effect a power to secure a monopoly of the Indian trade to himself and his friends.

As soon as General Bacon had marched to such a convenient distance from Jamestown that the Assembly thought they might deliberate with safety, the governor by their advice issued a proclamation of rebellion against him, commanding his followers to surrender him and forthwith disperse themselves. Not contented with this, he likewise gave orders at the same time for raising the militia of the country against him.

The people being much exasperated, and General Bacon by his address and eloquence having gained dominion over their hearts, they unanimously resolved that not a hair of his head should fall to the ground, much less that they should surrender him as a rebel. Therefore, they kept to their arms and instead of proceeding against the Indians they marched back to Jamestown, directing their fury against such of their friends and countrymen as should dare to oppose them.

The governor, seeing this, fled over the Bay to Accomac, whither he hoped the infection of Bacon's conspiracy had not reached. But there, instead of people's receiving him with open arms in remembrance of the former services he had done them, they began to make terms with him for redress of their grievances and for the ease and liberty of trade. Thus Sir William, who had been almost the idol of the people, was, by reason of the loyal part he acted, abandoned by all, except some few who went over to him from the western shore in sloops and boats, so that it was some time before he could make head against Bacon. But he left him to range through the country at discretion.

General Bacon at first held a convention of such of the chief gentlemen of the country as would come to him, especially of those about Middle Plantation [Williamsburg], who were near at hand. At this convention they made a declaration to justify his unlawful proceedings and obliged people to take an oath of obedience to him as their general. Then by their advice, on the pretense of the governor's abdication, he called an Assembly by writs signed by himself and four others of the Council.

By this time the governor had got together a small party to side with him. These he furnished with sloops, arms, and ammunition in order to cross the Bay and oppose the malcontents. By this means there happened some skirmishes in which several were killed and others taken prisoners. Thus they were going on by a civil war to destroy one another and lay waste their infant country when it pleased God, after some months' confusion, to put an end to their misfortunes as well as to Bacon's designs by his natural death.

He died at [Major Thomas Pate's] in Gloucester County, but where he was buried was never yet discovered, tho' afterwards there was great inquiry made with design to expose his bones to public infamy.

In the meanwhile, those disorders occasioned a general neglect of husbandry and a great destruction of the stocks, so that people had a dreadful prospect of want and famine. But the malcontents being thus disunited by the loss of their general in whom they all confided, they began to squabble among themselves, and every man's business was how to make the best terms he could find for himself.

Lieutenant General Ingram (whose true name was Johnson) and Major General Wakelett surrendered on condition of pardon for themselves and their followers, tho' they were both forced to submit to an incapacity of bearing office in that country for the future.

Peace being thus restored, Sir William Berkeley returned to his former seat of government and every man to his several habitation.

While this intestine war was fomenting there, the agents of the country in England could not succeed in their remonstrance against the propriety grants, tho' they were told that those grants should be revoked. But the news of their civil war reaching England about the same time, the king would then proceed no further in that matter; so the agents thought it their best way to compound with the proprietors. Accordingly, they agreed with them for four hundred pounds a man, which was paid, and so all the clamor against those grants ended; neither was there any more heard of them there till above a dozen years afterwards.

When this storm occasioned by Bacon was blown over and all things quiet again, Sir William Berkeley called an Assembly for settling the affairs of the country and for making reparation to such as had been oppressed. After which a regiment of soldiers arrived from England, which were sent to suppress the insurrection; but they coming after the business was over had no occasion to exercise their courage. However, they were kept on foot there about three years after, and in the Lord Culpeper's time paid off and disbanded.

After the agents had compounded with the proprietors, they obtained a new charter of the king, by which he confirmed to that country their former constitution with full assurance that they should forever after remain under the protection of his Majesty and his successors and always hold their lands immediately from the Crown.

The confusion occasioned by the civil war and the advantage the Indians made of it in butchering the English upon all their frontiers caused such a desolation and put the country so far back that to this day they have seated very little beyond the boundaries that were then inhabited. At that time Jamestown was again burnt down to the ground by Richard Lawrence, one of Bacon's captains, who, when his own men, that abhorred such barbarity, refused to obey his command, he himself became the executioner and fired the houses with his own hands.

(This unhappy town did never after arrive at the perfection it then had, and now it is almost deserted by the wild project of Governor Nicholson, who procured that the Assembly and general court should be removed from thence to Williamsburg, an inland place about seven miles from it.)

With the regiment above mentioned arrived commissioners to inquire into the occasion and authors of this rebellion; and Sir William Berkeley came to England, where from the time of his arrival his sickness obliged him to keep his chamber till he died, so that he had no opportunity of kissing the king's hand. But his Majesty declared himself well satisfied with his conduct in Virginia and was very kind to him during his sickness, often inquiring after his health and commanding him not to hazard it by too early an endeavor to come to court.

Upon Sir William Berkeley's voyage to England, Herbert Jeffreys, esquire, was appointed governor. He made formal articles of peace with the Indians and held an Assembly at Middle Plantation, wherein they settled and allowed a free trade with the Indians, but restrained it to certain marts to which the Indians should bring their commodities; and this also to be under such certain rules as were by that Assembly directed. But this method was not agreeable to the Indians, who had never before been under any regulation. They thought that if all former usages were not restored, the peace was not perfect and therefore did not much rely upon it, which made those new restrictions useless.

His time was very short there, he being taken off by death the year following. After him Sir Henry Chicheley was made deputy governor in the latter end of the year 1678. In his time the Assembly for the greater terror of the Indians built magazines at the heads of the four great rivers and furnished them with arms, ammunition, and men in constant service.

This Assembly also prohibited the importation of tobacco, which Carolina and sometimes Maryland were wont to send thither in order to its being shipped off for England. But in that, I think, Virginia mistook her interest, for had they permitted this custom to become habitual and thus engrossed the shipping, as would soon have happened, they could easily have regulated the trade of tobacco at any time without the concurrence of those other colonies and without submitting to their perverse humors as formerly.

The spring following Thomas Lord Culpeper arrived there [as] governor and carried with him some laws which had been drawn up in England to be enacted in their Assembly. In these he had the art of mixing the good of the country with his own particular interest, which was a sure means of getting them passed. And coming with the advantage of restoring peace to a troubled nation, it was not difficult for him to obtain whatever he pleased from the people. His influence, too, was the greater by the power he had of pardoning those who had a hand in the disorders committed in the late rebellion.

In his first Assembly he passed several acts very obliging to the country, viz., first, an Act of Naturalization, whereby the power of naturalizing foreigners was placed in the governor; secondly, an Act for Cohabitation and Encouragement of Trade and Manufactures, whereby a certain place in each county was appointed for a town in which all goods imported and exported were to be landed and shipped off, bought and sold (which act was kindly brought to nothing by the opposition of the merchants of London); thirdly, an Act of General Pardon and Oblivion, whereby all the transgressions and outrages committed in the time of the late rebellion were entirely remitted and reparation allowed to people that should be evil spoken of on that account.

But he put a sting into the tail of this law that justifies oppression whenever the people happen to fall into the hands of an ill governor. I mean the clause that imposes a penalty of five hundred pounds and a year's imprisonment upon any man that shall presume to speak disrespectfully of the governor. This is such a safeguard to tyranny, that let a governor commit never so many abuses, no person while he is there dare say a word against him, nor so much as go about to represent it to the throne of England for redress, for fear of incurring this severe penalty.

The same law also gives one hundred pounds and three months' imprisonment without bail for daring to speak or write disrespectfully of any one of the Council or of any judge or other principal officer in the country.

Although this law was at first intended merely to suppress rebellion and to pacify and reconcile the people one towards another—and no governor hath ever thought fit to put that clause in execution—yet it has of late been trumped up in revenge of personal injuries and for support of the heavy mismanagements which the country now groans under.

By passing some laws that obliged the country, the Lord Culpeper carried one that was very pleasing to himself, viz., the act for raising a public revenue for the better support of the government. By this he got the duties contained therein to be made perpetual, and that the money which before used to be accounted for to the Assembly should be from thenceforth disposed of by his Majesty's sole direction for the support of the government. When this was done, he obtained of the king a salary of two thousand pounds per annum instead of one thousand, which was formerly allowed; also 150 pounds per annum for house rent, besides all the usual perquisites.

In those submissive times his Lordship reduced the greatest perquisite of his place to a certainty, which before that was only gratuitous; that is, instead of the masters of ships making presents of liquors or provisions towards the governor's housekeeping, as they were wont to do, he demanded a certain sum of money, remitting that custom. This rate has ever since been demanded of all commanders as a duty, and is twenty shillings for each ship or vessel under a hundred tons, and thirty shillings for each ship upwards of that burden, to be paid every voyage or port clearing.

This noble lord was skillful in all the ways of getting money, and never let slip any opportunity of doing it. To this end he seemed to lament the unhappy state of the country in relation to their coin. He was tenderly concerned that all their cash should be drained away by the neighboring colonies, which had not set so low an estimate upon it as Virginia, and therefore he proposed the raising of it.

This was what the country had formerly desired, and the Assembly was at that time making a law for it; but his lordship stopped them, alleging it was the king's prerogative, by virtue of which he would do it by proclamation. This they did not approve of, well knowing if that were the case his lordship and every other governor would at any time have the same prerogative of altering it, and so people should never be at any certainty, as they quickly after found from his own practice. For his drift in all this proceeding, tho' gilded over with an affected kindness to the country, was only to make advantage of paying the soldiers, the money for that purpose being put into his lordship's hands. He had prudently provided light pieces of eight, which he with this view had bought at a cheap rate. When his contrivance was ripe for execution, he extended the royal prerogatives and issued forth a proclamation for raising the value of pieces of eight from five to six shillings; and as soon as they were admitted current at that value, he produced an order for paying and disbanding the soldiers. Then those poor fellows and such as had maintained them were forced to take their pay in those light pieces of eight at six shillings. But his lordship soon after himself found the inconvenience of that proclamation, for people began to pay their duties and their ship money in coin of that high estimate, which was like to cut short both his lordship's salary and perquisites, and so he was forced to make use of the same prerogative to reduce the money again to its former standard.

According to this despotic way of government, this noble lord tried another experiment in the tender part of their constitution, but did it so cautiously that it seemed to take off all reflection.

He put out a proclamation to repeal several laws which had been made since Bacon's Rebellion, but all of them related to the transactions of Bacon's time and were virtually, tho' not expressly, repealed by the Act of Indemnity and Oblivion.

However, this arbitrary method of doing business had like to have had a very unhappy effect, insomuch that if the late misfortunes of Bacon had not been so fresh in memory, it might perhaps have occasioned a new commotion. For at this rate of proceeding people looked upon their acts of Assembly to be of no more force than the laws of an Ottoman province which are liable to be suspended or repealed at the pleasure of the bashaw. In short, it bred such a mutiny in the country that the succeeding Assembly was forced to make a particular law to provide against the ill consequences of it.

Some few instances of repealing acts of Assembly after this absolute manner were also attempted in the time of the Lord Effingham's government. But notwithstanding his proclamation, the laws thereby pretended to be repealed are allowed to be of as great force in all courts of justice as they were before those proclamations, the law for paying the quitrent only excepted. This law allowed them to pay quitrents in tobacco at twopence per pound, but tobacco after that falling low, the proclamation repealed that law and demanded the payment in money according to the tenor of their patents, or else in tobacco at one penny per pound. And this imposition has been generally submitted to rather than any single man would stand a lawsuit against a governor, especially seeing that by the words of his patent the quitrent was reserved in money.

Afterwards Colonel Nicholson, when he was lieutenant governor under the same Lord Effingham, among the many arbitrary proceedings which he boasts to have learned formerly in the kingdom of Morocco, was pleased by his proclamation officiously to repeal a law which had been before repealed to his hand by another law. And these are all the attempts that have been made in that colony of the French method of governing by edicts.

In less than a year the Lord Culpeper returned to England, leaving Sir Henry Chicheley deputy governor.

The country being then settled again made too much tobacco for the market, and the merchants would hardly allow the planter anything for it.

This occasioned much uneasiness again, and the people, from former experience despairing of succeeding in any agreement with the neighboring governments, resolved a total destruction of the tobacco in that country, especially of the sweet-scented, because that was planted nowhere else. In pursuance of which design they contrived that all the plants should be destroyed while they were yet in the beds and after it was too late to sow more.

Accordingly, the ringleaders in this project began with their own first, and then went to cut up the plants of such of their neighbors as were not willing to do it themselves; however, they had not resolution enough to go through with their work.

This was adjudged sedition and felony. Several people were committed upon it, and some condemned to be hanged. And afterwards the Assembly passed a law to make such proceedings felony for the future.

After this accident of plant cutting, the Lord Culpeper returned and held his second Assembly in which he contrived to gain another great advantage over the country. His lordship in his first voyage thither, perceiving how easily he could twist and manage the people, conceived new hopes of retrieving the propriety of the Northern Neck, as being so small a part of the colony. He conceived that while the remainder escaped free, which was far the greater part, they would not engage in the interest of the lesser number, especially considering the discouragements they had met with before in their former solicitation; tho' all this while and for many years afterwards his lordship did not pretend to lay public claim to any part of the propriety.

It did not square with this project that appeals should be made to the General Assembly, as till then had been the custom. He feared the burgesses would be too much in the interest of their countrymen and adjudge the inhabitants of the Northern Neck to have an equal liberty and privilege in their estates with the rest of Virginia as being settled upon the same foot. In order, therefore, to make a better pennyworth of those poor people, he studied to overturn this odious method of appealing and to fix the last resort in another court that might judge more favorably of his unrighteous patents.

To bring this point about, his lordship contrived to blow up a difference in the Assembly between the Council and the burgesses, privately encouraging the burgesses to insist upon the privilege of determining all appeals by themselves exclusive of the Council, because they having given their opinions before in the general court, were for that reason unfit judges in appeals from themselves to the Assembly. This succeeded according to his wish, and the burgesses bit at the bait under the notion of privilege, never dreaming of the snake that lay in the grass nor considering the danger of altering an old constitution so abruptly. Thus that cunning lord gained his end, for he represented that quarrel with so many aggravations that he got an instruction from the king to take away all appeals from the general court to the Assembly and cause them to be made to himself in Council.

Of this his lordship made sufficient advantage, for in the confusion that happened in the end of King James II's reign, viz., October, 1688, he got an assignment from the other patentees and gained a favorable report from the king's Council upon his patent for the Northern Neck.

When he had succeeded in this, his lordship's next step was to engage some noted inhabitants of the place to be on his side.

Accordingly, he made use of his cousin, Secretary Spencer, who lived in the said Neck. This gentleman did but little in his lordship's service and only gained some few strays that used to be claimed by the coroner in behalf of the king.

Upon the death of Mr. Secretary Spencer, he engaged another noted gentleman, an old stander in that country, Colonel Philip Ludwell, who was then in England. He went over with this grant in the year 1690 and set up an office in the Neck, claiming some escheats, but he likewise could make nothing of it. After him Colonel George Brent and Colonel William Fitzhugh, that were likewise inhabitants of the said Neck, were employed in that affair, but succeeded no better than their predecessors. The people in the meanwhile complained frequently to their Assemblies, who at last made another address to the king; but there being no agent in England to prosecute it, that likewise miscarried. At last Colonel Richard Lee, one of the Council, an inhabitant of the Northern Neck, privately made a composition with the proprietors themselves for his own land. This broke the ice, and several were induced to follow so great an example, so that by degrees they were generally brought to pay their quitrents into the hands of the proprietors' agents. And now at last it is managed for them by Colonel Robert Carter, another of the Council and one of the greatest freeholders of that propriety.

To return to my Lord Culpeper's government, I cannot omit a useful thing which his lordship was pleased to do with relation to their courts of justice. It seems nicety of pleading, with all the juggle of Westminster Hall, was creeping into their courts. The clerks began in some cases to enter the reasons with the judgments, pretending to set precedents of inviolable form to be observed in all future proceedings. This my lord found fault with and retrenched all dilatory pleas as prejudicial to justice, keeping the courts close to the merits of the cause in order to bring it to a speedy determination, according to the innocence of former times. He caused the judgments to be entered up short without the reasons, alleging that their courts were not of so great experience as to be able to make precedents to posterity, who ought to be left at liberty to determine according to the equity of the controversy before them.

In his time also were dismantled the forts built by Sir Henry

Chicheley at the heads of the rivers, and the forces there were disbanded as being too great a charge. The Assembly appointed small parties of light horse in their stead to range by turns upon the frontiers. These, being chosen out of the neighboring inhabitants, might afford to serve at easier rates and yet do the business more effectually.

After this the Lord Culpeper returned again for England, his second stay not being much longer than the first; and Sir Henry Chicheley being dead, he irregularly proclaimed his kinsman, Mr. Secretary Spencer, president, tho' he was not the eldest member of the Council.

The next year being 1684, upon the Lord Culpeper's refusing to return, Francis Lord Howard Effingham was sent over governor. This noble lord had as great an affection for money as his predecessor, and made it his business to equip himself with as much of it as he could without respect either to the laws of the plantation or the dignity of his office. His lordship condescended to share with his clerk the meaner profits of ministerial offices; and to serve this turn the more effectually, he imposed the charge of a license under seal on all schoolmasters for teaching of children and on all practitioners at the bar for pleading. He also extorted an excessive fee for putting the seal to all probates of wills and letters of administration, even where the estates of the deceased were of the meanest value. Neither could any be favored with such administration or probate without paying that extortion. If anybody presumed to remonstrate against it, his lordship's behavior towards that man was very severe. He kept several persons in prison and under confinement from court to court without bringing them to trial, which proceedings and many others were so oppressive that complaints were made thereof to the king, and Colonel Philip Ludwell was appointed agent to appear against him in England. And tho' Colonel Ludwell had not the good fortune to get his lordship turned out, yet his indefatigable application in that affair deserves an honorable commemoration.

During the first session of Assembly in this noble lord's time, the duty on liquors imported from the other English plantations was first imposed. It was then laid on pretense of lessening the levy by the poll for payment of public taxes, but more especially for rebuilding the State House, which had not been rebuilt since Lawrence burnt it in Bacon's time.

This duty was at first laid on wine and rum only at the rate of threepence per gallon with an exemption of all such as should be imported in the ships of Virginia owners. But the like duty has since been laid on other liquors also, and is raised to fourpence per gallon on wine and rum and one penny per gallon on beer, cider, lime juice, etc., and the privilege of Virginia owners is quite taken away to the great discouragement of their shipping and home trade.

This lord, though he pretended to no great skill in legal proceedings, yet he made great innovations in their courts, pretending to follow the English forms; thus he created a new court of chancery distinct from the general court, who had ever before claimed that jurisdiction. He erected himself into a Lord Chancellor, taking the gentlemen of the Council to sit with him as mere associates and advisers, not having any vote in the causes before them. And that it might have more the air of a new court, he would not so much as sit in the State House, where all the other public business was dispatched, but took the dining room of a private house for that use. He likewise made arbitrary tables of fees peculiar to this high court. However, his lordship not beginning this project very long before he left the country, all these innovations came to an end upon his removal, and the jurisdictions returned to the general court again in the time of Colonel Nathaniel Bacon [cousin of the rebel] whom he left president.

During that gentleman's presidency, which began anno 1689, the project of a college was first agreed upon. The contrivers drew up their scheme and presented it to the president and Council. This was by them approved and referred to the next Assembly. But Colonel Bacon's administration being very short and no Assembly called all the while, this pious design could proceed no further.

Anno 1690: Francis Nicholson, esquire, being appointed lieutenant governor under the Lord Effingham, arrived there. This gentleman's business was to fix himself in my lord's place and recommend himself to the supreme government. For that end he studied popularity, discoursing freely of country improvements.

He made his court to the people by instituting Olympic games and giving prizes to all those that should excel in the exercises of riding, running, shooting, wrestling, and backsword. When the design of a college was communicated to him, he foresaw what interest it might create him with the bishops in England, and therefore promised it all imaginable encouragement. The first thing desired of him in its behalf was the calling of an Assembly, but this he would by no means agree to, being under obligations to the Lord Effingham to stave off Assemblies as long as he could for fear there might be further representations sent over against his lordship, who was conscious to himself how uneasy the country had been under his despotic administration.

When that could not be obtained, then they proposed that a subscription might pass thro' the colony to try the humor of the people in general and see what voluntary contributions they could get towards it. This he granted, and he himself together with the Council set a generous example to the other gentlemen of the country, so that the subscriptions at last amounted to about £2,500, in which sum is included the generous benevolences of several merchants of London.

Anno 1691: An Assembly being called, this design was moved to them, and they espoused it heartily and soon after made an address to King William and Queen Mary in its behalf and sent the Reverend Mr. James Blair their agent to England to solicit their Majesties' charter for it.

It was proposed that three things should be taught in this college, viz., languages, divinity, and natural philosophy.

They appointed a certain number of professors and their salaries.

And they formed rules for the continuation and good government thereof to perpetuity. But of this I shall speak more particularly in the last part of my book, wherein the present state will be considered.

The Assembly was so fond of Governor Nicholson at that time that they presented him with the sum of three hundred pounds as a testimony of their good disposition towards him. But he having an instruction to receive no present from the country, they drew up an address to their Majesties praying that he might have leave to accept it.

This he took an effectual way to secure by making a promise that if their Majesties would please to permit him to accept it, he would give one half thereof to the college; and so he secured at once both the money and the character of being a generous person.

Their Majesties were well pleased with that pious design of the plantation and granted a charter according to their desire; in obtaining which the address and assiduity of Mr. Blair, their agent, was highly to be admired.

Their Majesties were graciously pleased to give near two thousand pounds sterling, the balance due upon the account of quitrents, towards the founding the college; and towards the endowing of it they allowed twenty thousand acres of choice land, together with the revenue arising by the penny per pound on tobacco exported from Virginia and Maryland to other plantations.

It was a great satisfaction to the archbishops and bishops to see such a nursery of religion founded in that New World, especially for that it was begun in an episcopal way and carried on wholly by zealous conformists to the Church of England.

In this first Assembly, Lieutenant Governor Nicholson passed acts for the encouragement of linen manufacture and to promote the leather trade by tanning, currying, and shoemaking. He also in that session passed a law for cohabitation and improvement of trade.

In the general court he was a strict observer of the acts of Assembly, making them the sole rule of his judgment wherever they happened not to be silent.

But his behavior in Council at the same time did not square with that regularity, for there he was so arbitrary and imperious that they could not bear it, and several of the councilors writ letters to the court of England against him; where instead of giving redress to their grievances they sent their original letters back to him.

Before the next Assembly he tacked about and was quite the reverse of what he was in the first. Instead of encouraging ports and towns, he spread abroad his dislike of them, and went among the people finding fault with those things which he and the Assembly had unanimously agreed upon the preceding session. Such a violent change there was in him that it surprised everybody at first, but they soon found out that it proceeded from some other cause than barely the inconstancy of his temper. Of this last opinion he continued till his removal, which happened soon after.

In February, 1692, Sir Edmund Andros arrived governor. He began his government with an Assembly which overthrew the good design of ports and towns (but the groundwork of this proceeding was laid before Sir Edmund's arrival). However, this Assembly proceeded no further than to suspend the law till their Majesties' pleasure should be known. But it seems the merchants in London were dissatisfied and made public complaints against it, which their Majesties were pleased to hear, and afterwards referred the law back to the Assembly again to consider if it were suitable to the circumstances of the country and to regulate it accordingly. But the Assembly never proceeded any further in it, and so it lies at this day.

Sir Edmund Andros by a mistaken zeal brought an innovation into their courts which was a hardship upon the country. He caused all the statutes of England, even those made since their last charter—notwithstanding they did not mention the plantations, even such as particularly related to usages and customs peculiar to England—to be law in their courts. He set up the statutes of England to be the sole rule of his judgment, as the lieutenant governor had made the acts of Assembly of his. This gave them a new distraction, so that they knew not what was law nor when they were secure in their estates. He was likewise frequently pleased to say they had no title to their lands, for a reason which neither himself nor anybody else knew. These things caused great heartburnings in his time.

With Sir Edmund Andros was sent over the college charter, and the subsequent Assembly declared that the subscriptions which had been made to the College were due and immediately demandable. They likewise gave a duty on the exportation of skins and furs for its more plentiful endowment.

The subscription money did not come in with the same readiness with which it had been underwritten. However, there was enough given by their Majesties and gathered from the people to keep all hands at work and carry on the building; the foundation whereof they then laid.

Sir Edmund Andros was a great encourager of manufactures. In his time fulling mills were set up by act of Assembly. He also gave particular marks of his favor towards the propagating of cotton, which since his time has been much neglected. He was likewise a great lover of method and dispatch in all sorts of business, which made him find fault with the management of the secretary's office. And, indeed, with very good reason; for from the time of Bacon's Rebellion till then, there never was any office in the world more negligently kept. Several patents of land were entered blank upon record; many original patents, records, and deeds of land, with other matters of great consequence, were thrown loose about the office and suffered to be dirted, torn, and eaten by the moths and other insects. But upon this gentleman's accession to the government, he immediately gave directions to reform all these irregularities. He caused the loose and torn records of value to be transcribed into new books and ordered conveniences to be built within the office for preserving the records from being lost and confounded as before. He prescribed methods to keep the papers dry and clean and to reduce them into such order as that anything might be turned to immediately. But all these conveniencies were burnt soon after they were finished, in October, 1698, together with the office itself and the whole State House. But his diligence was so great in that affair that tho' his stay afterwards in the country was very short, yet he caused all the records and papers which had been saved from the fire to be sorted again and registered in order, and, indeed, in much better order than ever they had been before. In this condition he left 'em at his quitting the government.

He made several offers to rebuild the State House in the same place, and had his government continued but six months longer 'tis probable he would have effected it after such a manner as might have been least burdensome to the people.

In November, 1698, Francis Nicholson, esquire, was removed from Maryland to be governor of Virginia. But he went not then with that smoothness on his brow he had carried with him when he was appointed lieutenant governor. He talked then no more of improving of manufactures, towns, and trade; neither was he pleased to make the acts of Assembly the rule of his judgments as formerly, but his own all-sufficient will and pleasure. Instead of encouraging the manufactures, he sent over inhuman memorials against them which were so opposite to all reason that they refuted themselves. In one of these he remonstrates "that the tobacco of that country often bears so low a price that it will not yield clothes to the people that make it"; and yet presently after in the same memorial he recommends it to the Parliament "to pass an act forbidding the plantations to make their own clothing," which, in other words, *is desiring a charitable law that the planters shall go naked.* In a late memorial concerted between him and his creature Colonel Quarry 'tis most humbly proposed "that all the English colonies on the continent of North America be reduced under one government and under one viceroy, and that a standing army be there kept on foot to subdue the queen's enemies," which in plain English is imploring her Majesty to put the plantations under martial law and in the consequence to give the viceroy a fair opportunity of shaking off his dependence upon England.

He began his government with a pompous show of zeal for the Church, tho' his practice was not of a piece with his pious pretensions. It must be confessed that he has bestowed some liberalities upon the clergy, but always upon condition that they should proclaim his charity either by signing addresses dictated by himself in his own commendation or at least by writing letters of it to the bishops in England. And he would ever be so careful to hinder these representations from miscarrying that he constantly took copies of them and sent 'em with his own letters.

He likewise gave himself airs of encouraging the College, but he used this pretext for so many by-ends that at last the promoters of that good work grew weary of the mockery. They perceived his view was to gain himself a character, and if he could but raise that, the College might sink. And in truth he has been so far from advancing it that now after six years of his government the scholars are fewer than at his arrival.

Soon after his accession to the government he caused the Assembly and courts of judicature to be removed from Jamestown where there were good accommodations for people to Middle

Plantation where there were none. There he flattered himself with the fond imagination of being the founder of a new city. He marked out the streets in many places so as that they might represent the figure of a W in memory of his late Majesty King William, after whose name the town was called Williamsburg. There he procured a stately fabric to be erected which he placed opposite to the College and graced it with the magnificent name of the capitol.

This imaginary city is yet advanced no further than only to have a few public houses and a storehouse more than were built upon the place before. And by the frequency of public meetings and the misfortune of his residence the students are interrupted in their study and make less advances than formerly.

To defray the charge of building the capitol he suggested the pernicious duty of fifteen shillings for each Christian servant imported, except English, and twenty shillings for each Negro. I call this a pernicious duty because 'tis a great hindrance to the increase of that young colony as well as a very unequal tax upon their labor.

It has been the constant maxim of this gentleman to set the people at variance as much as possible amongst themselves. Whether this proceed from his great fondness to the Machiavellian principle *"divide et impera,"* or from his exceeding good nature, I won't pretend to determine. But 'tis very certain that by his management he has divided the most friendly and most united people in the world into very unhappy factions. And what is still worse, he has been heard to declare publicly to the populace "that the gentlemen imposed upon them and that the servants had been all kidnapped and had a lawful action against their masters."

And that these things may make the more effectual impression, he takes care to vilify the gentlemen of the Council in public places by the grossest and most injurious language. He is frequently pleased to send vexatious commands to summon people in her Majesty's name to attend him at some general meeting, and when they come all the business perhaps he has with them is to affront them before all the company.

In the general court, of which he is chief judge, he has often behaved himself in that boisterous manner that neither the rest of the judges on the bench nor the lawyers at the bar could use their just freedom. There 'tis usual with him to fall into excessive passions and utter the most abusive language against those that presume to oppose his arbitrary proceedings. If the attorney general be so scrupulous as to excuse himself from executing his illegal commands, he runs a great risk of being ill used. For in the year 1700, Mr. Fowler, who was then the king's attorney, declining some hard piece of service as being against the law, his Excellency in a fury took him by the collar and swore that he knew of no laws they had, and that his commands should be obeyed without hesitation or reserve. He often commits gentlemen to jail without the least shadow of complaint against them, and that without bail or mainprize to the great oppression of the queen's loyal subjects. Some of those have taken the liberty to tell him that such proceedings were illegal and not to be justified in any country that had the happiness to be governed by the laws of England. To whom he has been heard to reply that "they had no right at all to the liberties of *English* subjects, and that he would hang up those that should presume to oppose him with Magna Charta about their necks."

He often mentions the absolute government of Fez and Morocco with great pleasure and extols the inhuman cruelties of that prince towards his subjects. And particularly one day at a meeting of the governors of the College, upon some opposition they made against one of his violent proceedings, he vouchsafed to tell them that "they were dogs and their wives were bitches, that he knew how to govern the *Moors* and would beat them into better manners."

Neither does this gentleman treat the Assemblies with more gentleness than particular people, for he has said very publicly "that he knew how to govern the country without Assemblies, and if they should deny him anything after he had obtained a standing army, he would bring them to reason with halters about their necks."

But no wonder that he deals so freely with the people there, since neither her Majesty's instructions nor the laws of that country can restrain him. Thus he takes upon him to transact matters of the greatest moment without advice of the Council; as for example, he has appointed several officers without their advice, which he ought not to do. Sometimes he has brought his orders in his hand into the Council and signed them at the board without so much as acquainting the Council what they were, tho' at the same time they ought not to pass without their advice; and after he had done this, he ordered the clerk to enter them into the minutes as if they had been acted by the consent of the Council.

If any of the Council happen to argue or vote anything contrary to this gentleman's inclinations, he instantly flies out into the most outrageous passions and treats them with terms very unbecoming his station. By this means he takes away all freedom of debate and makes the Council of no other use than to palliate his arbitrary practices. Sometimes when he finds he can't carry matters there as he desires, he makes no scruple of entering them in the Council books by his own authority; he likewise causes many things to be erased out and others put in by his own absolute will and pleasure. Nay, sometimes too, he has caused an abstract of the journals to be sent to England instead of the journals themselves, by which artifice he leaves out or puts in just as much as he thinks fit.

He is very sensible how unwarrantable and unjust these proceedings are, and therefore has been always jealous lest some of the many that have been injured should send over their complaints to England. This has put him upon a practice most destructive to all trade and correspondence, which is the intercepting and breaking open of letters. His method was to give directions to some of his creatures dwelling near the mouths of the rivers to send on board the several ships that happened to arrive, and in the governor's name demand the letters. Thus he used to get them and open as many as he thought fit, after which sometimes he would cause 'em to be sent where they were directed and sometimes keep them. By this management many people have not only suffered the loss of their letters and of their accounts, invoices, etc., but likewise have missed great advantages for want of timely advice, occasioned by the stopping of their letters.

Another effect of his jealousy was to set spies upon such people as he suspected. These were to give him an account of all the words and actions of those which were most likely to complain; nay, his Excellency has condescended to act the low part of an eavesdropper himself and to stand under a window to listen for secrets that would certainly displease him. This practice has made every man afraid of his neighbor and destroyed the mutual confidence of the dearest friends.

But the most extraordinary method of learning secrets that ever was used in an English government was a kind of inquisition which this gentleman has been pleased to erect frequently in that country. He would call courts at unusual times to inquire into the life and conversation of those persons that had the misfortune to be out of his favor, tho' there was not the least public accusation against them. To these courts he summoned all the neighbors of the party he intended to expose, especially those that he knew were most intimate with him. Upon their appearance he administered an oath to them to answer truly to all such interrogatories as he should propose. Then he would ask them endless questions concerning the particular discourse and behavior of the party in order to find out something that might be the ground of an accusation.

In the second year of this gentleman's government, there happened an adventure very fortunate for him which gave him much credit with those who relied on his own account of the matter; and that was the taking of a pirate within the capes of that country.

It fell out that several merchant ships were got ready and fallen down to Lynhaven Bay, near the mouth of James River, in order for sailing. A pirate being informed of this, and hearing that there was no man-of-war there except a sixth-rate, ventured within the capes and took several of the merchant ships. But a small vessel happened to come down the Bay, and seeing an engagement between the pirate and a merchantman, made a shift to get into the mouth of James River, where the *Shoram*, a fifth-rate man-of-war, was newly arrived. The sixth-rate, commanded by Captain John Aldred, was then on the carine in Elizabeth River in order for her return to England.

The governor happened to be at that time at Kiquotan sealing up his letters, and Captain Passenger, commander of the *Shoram*, went ashore to pay his respects to him. In the meanwhile news was brought that a pirate was got within the capes, upon which the captain was in haste to go aboard his ship; but the governor would have stayed him, promising to go along with him. The captain soon after asked his excuse and went off, leaving him another boat if he pleased to follow. It was about one o'clock in the afternoon when the news was brought, but 'twas within night before his Excellency went aboard, staying all that while ashore upon some weighty pretenses. However, at last he followed, and by break of day the man-of-war was fairly out between the capes and the pirate, where, after ten hours' sharp engagement, the pirate was obliged to strike and surrender upon the terms of being left to the king's mercy.

Now it happened that three men of this pirate's gang were not on board their own ship at the time of the surrender and so were not included in the articles of capitulation but were tried in that country. In summing up the charge against them (the governor being present), the attorney general extolled his Excellency's mighty courage and conduct as if the honor of taking the pirate had been due to him. Upon this, Captain Passenger took the freedom to interrupt Mr. Attorney in open court and said that he was commander of the *Shoram*, that the pirates were his prisoners, and that nobody had pretended to command in that engagement but himself. He further desired that the governor would do him the justice to confess whether he had given the least word of command all that day or directed any one thing during the whole fight. Upon this, his Excellency tamely acknowledged that what the captain said was true and so fairly yielded him all the honor of that exploit.

This governor likewise gained some reputation by another instance of his management, whereby he has let the world know the violent passion he has to publish his own fame.

He had zealously recommended to the court of England the necessity that Virginia should contribute a certain quota of men or else a sum of money towards the building and maintaining a fort at New York. The reason he gave for this was because New York was their barrier and as such it was but justice they should help defend it. This was by order of his late Majesty King William proposed to the Assembly; but upon the most solid reasons they humbly remonstrated *that neither the forts then in being nor any other that might be built in the province of New York could in the least avail to the defense and security of Virginia, for that either the French or the Indians might invade that colony and not come within a hundred miles of any such fort.* The truth of these objections is obvious to anyone that ever looked on the maps of that part of the world. But the secret of the whole business in plain terms was this: those forts were necessary for New York to enable that province to engross the trade of the neighbor Indians, which being highly to the disadvantage of Virginia 'twas unreasonable that country should pay a tribute towards its own ruin. And since New York would reap all the benefit of such forts, 'twas but just it should bear all the charge of building them.

Now the glory Colonel Nicholson got in that affair was this: after he had represented Virginia as republican and rebellious for not complying with his proposal, he said publicly that New York should not want the nine hundred pounds tho' he paid it out of his own pocket and soon after took a journey to that province.

When he arrived there he gave his own bills of exchange for nine hundred pounds to the aforesaid use, boasting that he only relied on her Majesty's goodness to reimburse him out of the quitrents of Virginia. But this was nothing but grimace, for at the same time that he passed the bills he prudently took a defeasance from the gentleman to whom they were given, specifying *that till her Majesty should be graciously pleased to remit him the money out of the quitrents, those bills should never be made use of.* This was an admirable piece of sham generosity and worthy of the great pains he took to proclaim it. I myself have frequently heard him boast that he gave this money out of his own pocket and only depended on the queen's bounty to repay him.

Neither was he contented to spread abroad this untruth there, but he also foisted it into a memorial of Colonel Quarry's to the Council of Trade in which are these words: "As soon as Governor Nicholson found the Assembly of Virginia would not see their own interest nor comply with her Majesty's orders, he went immediately to New York, and out of his great zeal to the queen's service and the security of her province he gave his own bills for nine hundred pounds to answer the quota of Virginia, wholly depending on her Majesty's favor to reimburse him out of the revenues in that province."

Certainly his Excellency and Colonel Quarry, by whose joint wisdom and sincerity this memorial was composed, must believe that the Council of Trade have very imperfect intelligence how matters pass in that part of the world, or else they would not presume to impose such a banter upon them.

But this is nothing if compared to some other passages of that unjust representation, wherein they take upon them to describe the people of Virginia "to be both numerous and rich, of republican notions and principles such as ought to be corrected and lowered in time; and that now or never is the only time to maintain the queen's prerogative and put a stop to those wrong pernicious notions which are improving daily, not only in Virginia but in all her Majesty's other governments. A frown now from her Majesty will do more than an army hereafter, etc."

With those inhuman reflections do those gentlemen afterwards introduce the necessity of a standing army, the truth of which is equal to that of the precedent paragraph. Thus are that loyal people privately and basely misrepresented because they struggle against the oppression which this governor practices in contempt of her Majesty's instructions and the laws of the country. But I challenge the authors of that memorial to give one single instance wherein the inhabitants of Virginia have shown the least want of loyalty to the queen or the least disaffection to England.

BOOK TWO

Of the Natural Product and Conveniences of Virginia in Its Unimproved State Before the English Went Thither

1

Of the Bounds and Coast of Virginia

Virginia, as you have heard before, was a name at first given to all the northern part of the continent of America, and when the original grant was made both to the first and second colonies—that is, to those of Virginia and New England—they were both granted under the name of Virginia. And afterwards, when grants for other new colonies were made by particular names, those names for a long time served only to distinguish them as so many parts of Virginia. And until the plantations became more familiar to England, it was so continued. But in process of time the name of Virginia was lost to all except to that tract of land lying along the Bay of Chesapeake and a little to the southward, in which are included Virginia and Maryland, both which, in common discourse, are still very often meant by the name of Virginia.

The entrance into Virginia for shipping is by the mouth of Chesapeake Bay, which is indeed more like a river than a bay, for it runs up into the land about two hundred miles, being everywhere near as wide as it is at the mouth and in many places much wider. The mouth thereof is about seven leagues over, through which all ships must pass to go to Maryland.

The coast is a bold and even coast with regular soundings and is open all the year round; so that having the latitude—which also can hardly be wanted—upon a coast where so much clear weather is, any ship may go in by soundings alone by day or night, in summer or winter, and need not fear any disaster if the mariners understand anything. For let the wind blow how it will and chop about as suddenly as it pleases, any master, tho' his ship be never so dull, has opportunity (by the evenness of the coast) either of standing off and clearing the shore or else of running into safe harbor within the capes. A bolder and safer coast is not known in the universe, to which conveniences there's the addition of good anchorage all along upon it without the capes.

Virginia, in the most restrained sense distinct from Maryland, is the spot to which I shall altogether confine this description; tho' you may consider at the same time that there cannot be much difference between this and Maryland, they being contiguous one to the other, lying in the same Bay, producing the same sort of commodities, and being fallen into the same unhappy form of settlements—altogether upon country seats without towns. Virginia thus considered is bounded on the south by North Carolina, on the north by Potomac River (which divides it from Maryland), on the east by the main ocean (called the Virginia Seas), and on the west and northwest by the California Sea, whenever the settlements shall be extended so far.

This part of Virginia now inhabited, if we consider the improvements in the hands of the English, it cannot upon that score be commended; but if we consider its natural aptitude to be improved, it may with justice be accounted one of the finest countries in the world. Most of the natural advantages of it, therefore, I shall endeavor to discover and set in their true light together with its inconveniences, and afterwards proceed to the improvements.

2

Of the Waters

The largeness of the Bay of Chesapeake I have mentioned already. From one end of it to the other there's good anchorage and so little danger of a wreck that many masters who have never been there before venture up to the head of the Bay upon the slender knowledge of a common sailor. But the experience of one voyage teaches any master to go up afterwards without a pilot.

Besides this Bay, the country is watered with four great rivers, viz., James, York, Rappahannock, and Potomac Rivers, all which are full of convenient and safe harbors. There are also abundance of lesser rivers, many of which are capable of receiving the biggest merchant ships.

These rivers are of such convenience that for almost every half dozen miles of their extent there's a commodious and safe road for a whole fleet, which gives opportunity to the masters of ships to lie up and down straggling, according as they have made their acquaintance, riding before that gentleman's door where they find the best reception or where 'tis most suitable to their business.

These rivers are made up by the conflux of an infinite number of crystal springs of cool and pleasant water issuing everywhere out of the banks and sides of the valleys. These springs flow so plentifully that they make the river water fresh fifty, three score, and sometimes a hundred miles below the flux and reflux of the tides, and sometimes within thirty or forty miles of the Bay itself. The conveniences of these springs are so many they are not to be numbered. I shall, therefore, content myself to mention that one [convenience] of supplying the country everywhere except in the lowlands with as many mills as they can find work for; and some of these send forth such a glut a water that in less than half a mile below the fountainhead they afford a stream sufficient to supply a gristmill, of which there are several instances.

The only mischief I know belonging to these rivers is that in the month of June annually there rise up in the salts vast beds of seedling worms, which enter the ships, sloops, or boats wherever they find the coat of pitch, tar, or lime worn off the timber, and by degrees eat the plank into cells like those of an honeycomb. These worms continue thus upon the surface of the water from their rise in June until the first great rains after the middle of July, but after that do no other damage till the next summer season, and never penetrate farther than the plank or timber they first fix upon.

3

Of the Earths and Soil

The soil is of such variety, according to the difference of situation, that one part or other of it seems fitted to every sort of plant that is requisite either for the benefit or pleasure of mankind. And were it not for the high mountains to the northwest, which are supposed to retain vast magazines of snow and by that means cause the wind from that quarter to descend a little too cold upon them, 'tis believed that many of those delicious summer fruits growing in the hotter climates might be kept there green all the winter without the charge of housing or any other care than what is due to the natural plants of the country when transplanted into a garden. But as that would be no considerable charge, any man that is curious might with all the ease imaginable preserve as many of them as would gratify a moderate luxury; and the summer affords genial heat enough to ripen them to perfection.

There are three different kinds of land, according to the difference of situation, either in the lower parts of the country, the middle, or that on the heads of the rivers.

1. The land towards the mouth of the rivers is generally of a low, moist, and fat mold, such as the heavier sort of grain delight in, as rice, hemp, Indian corn, etc. This also is varied here and there with veins of a cold, hungry, sandy soil of the same moisture and very often lying under water. But this also has its advantages, for on such land generally grow the huckleberries, cranberries, chinquapins, etc. These low lands are for the most part well stored with oaks, poplars, pines, cedars, cypress, and sweet gums, the trunks of which are often thirty, forty, some sixty or seventy foot high, without a branch or limb. They likewise produce great variety of evergreens, unknown to me by name, besides the beauteous holly, sweet myrtle, cedar, and the live oak, which for three-quarters of the year is continually dropping its acorns and at the same time budding and bearing others in their stead.

2. The land higher up the rivers throughout the whole country is generally a level ground with shallow valleys full of streams and pleasant springs of clear water, having interspersed here and there

among the large levels some small hills and extensive vales. The mold in some places is black, fat, and thick laid; in others looser, lighter, and thin. The foundation of the mold is also various: sometimes clay, then gravel and rocky stones, and sometimes marl. The middle of the necks or ridges between the rivers is generally poor, being either a light sand or a white or red clay with a thin mold; yet even these places are stored with chestnuts, chinquapins, acorns of the shrub oak, and a reedy grass in summer very good for cattle. The rich lands lie next the rivers and branches and are stored with large oaks, walnuts, hickories, ash, beech, poplar, and many other sorts of timber of surprising bigness.

3. The heads of the rivers afford a mixture of hills, valleys, and plains, some richer than other, whereof the fruits and timber trees are also various. In some places lie great plats of low and very rich ground, well timbered; in others large spots of meadows and savannas, wherein are hundreds of acres without any tree at all, but yield reeds and grass of incredible height. And in the swamps and sunken grounds grow trees as vastly big as I believe the world affords and stand so close together that the branches or boughs of many of them lock into one another; but what lessens their value is that the greatest bulk of them are at some distance from water carriage. The land of these upper parts affords greater variety of soil than any other and as great variety in the foundations of the soil, or mold of which good judgment may be made by the plants and herbs that grow upon it. The rivers and creeks do in many places form very fine, large marshes which are a convenient support for their flocks and herds.

There is likewise found great variety of earths for physic, cleansing, scouring, and making all sorts of potters' ware, such as antimony, talc, yellow and red ocher, fuller's earth, pipe clay, and other fat and fine clays, marl, etc. In a word, there are all kinds of earth fit for use.

They have besides in those upper parts coal for firing, slate for covering, and stones for building and flat paving in vast quantities, as likewise pebble stones. Nevertheless, it has been confidently affirmed by many who have been there that there is not a stone in all the country. If such travelers knew no better than they said, my judgment of them is that either they were people of extreme short memories or else of very narrow observation. For tho' generally the lower parts are flat and so free from stones that people seldom shoe their horses, yet in many places, and particularly near the falls of the rivers, are found vast quantities of stone fit for all kind of uses. However, as yet there is seldom any use made of them because commonly wood is to be had at much less trouble. And as for coals, it is not likely they should ever be used there in anything but forges and great towns, if ever they happen to have any; for in their country plantations the wood grows at every man's door so fast that after it has been cut down it will in seven years' time grow up again from seed to substantial firewood, and in eighteen or twenty years 'twill come to be very good board timber.

For mineral earths 'tis believed they have great plenty and variety, that country being in a good latitude and having great appearances of them. It has been proved, too, that they have both iron and lead, as appears by what was said before concerning the iron work set up at Falling Creek in James River, where the iron proved reasonably good. But before they got into the body of the mine the people were cut off in that fatal massacre, and the project has never been set on foot since. However, Colonel Byrd, who is proprietor of that land, is at this time boring and searching after the richest veins near the place of the former work which is very commodious for such an undertaking by reason of the neighborhood of abundance of wood, running water, firestone, and other necessaries for that purpose.

Some people that have been in that country without knowing anything about it have affirmed that it is all a flat without any mixture of hills, because they see the coast to seaward perfectly level. Or else they have made their judgment of the whole country by the lands lying on the lower parts of the river (which perhaps they had never been beyond) and so conclude it to be throughout plain and even. When in truth upon the heads of the great rivers there are vast high hills, and even among the settlements there are some so topping that I have stood upon them and viewed the country all around over the tops of the highest trees for many leagues together. Particularly, there are Mawborn hills in the freshes of James River, a ridge of hills about fourteen or fifteen miles up Mattapony River, Tolivers Mount upon Rappahannock River, and the ridge of hills in Stafford County in the freshes of Potomac

River—all which are within the bounds of the English inhabitants. But a little farther backward there are mountains which indeed deserve the name of mountains for their height and bigness. But since I have not seen them myself I shall not pretend to give an account of them.

These hills are not without their advantages, for out of almost every rising ground throughout the country there issue abundance of most pleasant streams of pure and crystal water, than which certainly the world does not afford any more delicious. These are everywhere to be found in the upper parts of this country, and many of them flow out of the sides of banks very high above the vales, which are the most suitable places for gardens; where the finest waterworks in the world may be made at a very small expense.

There are likewise several mineral springs easily discoverable by their taste, as well as by the soil which they drive out with their streams. But I am not naturalist skillful enough to describe them with the exactness they deserve.

4

Of the Wild Fruits
of the Country

Of fruits natural to the country there is great abundance, but the several species of them are produced according to the difference of the soil and the various situation of the country, it being impossible that one piece of ground should produce so many different kinds intermixed. Of the better sorts of the wild fruits that I have met with, I will barely give you the names, not designing a natural history. And when I have done that, possibly I may not mention one-half of what the country affords, because I never went out of my way to inquire after anything of this nature.

Of the stoned fruits I have met with three good sorts, viz., cherries, plums, and persimmons.

Of cherries natural to the country and growing wild in the woods, I have seen three sorts. Two of these grow upon trees as big as the common English white oak, whereof one grows in bunches like grapes. Both these sorts are black without, and but one of them red within. That which is red within is more palatable than the English black cherry, as being without its bitterness; the other, which hangs on the branch like grapes, is water-colored within, of a faintish sweet and greedily devoured by the small birds. The third sort is called the Indian cherry and grows higher up in the country than the others do. It is commonly found by the sides of rivers and branches on small slender trees scarce able to support themselves, about the bigness of the peach trees in England. This is certainly the most delicious cherry in the world. It is of a dark purple when ripe and grows upon a single stalk like the English cherry, but is very small, though I suppose it may be made larger by cultivation if anybody would mind it. These, too, are so greedily devoured by the small birds that they won't let them remain on the tree long enough to ripen, by which means they are rarely known to any and much more rarely tasted, though perhaps at the same time they grow just by the houses.

The plums which I have observed to grow wild there are of two sorts; the black and the murrey plum, both which are small and have much the same relish with the damasine [damson].

The persimmon is by Hariot called the Indian plum, and so Smith, Purchas, and de Laet call it after him, but I can't perceive that any of those authors had ever heard of the sorts I have just now mentioned, they growing high up in the country. These persimmons amongst them retain their Indian name. They are of several sizes, between the bigness of a damasine and a bergamot pear. The taste of them is so very rough it is not to be endured till they are fully ripe, and then they are a pleasant fruit. Of these some virtuosi make an agreeable kind of beer, to which purpose they dry them in cakes and lay them up for use. These, like most other fruits there, grow as thick upon the trees as ropes of onions; the branches very often break down by the mighty weight of the fruit.

Of berries there is a great variety, and all very good in their kinds. Our mulberries are of three sorts, two black and one white. The long black sort is the best, being about the bigness of a boy's thumb; the other two sorts are of the shape of the English mulberry, short and thick, but their taste does not so generally please, being of a faintish sweet without any tartness. They grow upon well spread, large bodied trees, which run up surprisingly fast. These are the proper food of the silkworm.

There grow naturally two sorts of currants, one red and the other black, far more pleasant than those of the same color in England. They grow upon small bushes.

There are three sorts of hurts, or huckleberries, upon bushes from two to ten foot high. They grow in the valleys and sunken grounds, having different relishes, but are all pleasing to the taste. The largest sort grow upon the largest bushes, and I think are the best berries.

Cranberries grow in the low lands and barren sunken grounds upon low bushes, like the gooseberry, and are much of the same size. They are of a lively red when ripe and make very good tarts. I believe these are the berries which Captain Smith compared to the English gooseberry and called "raxcomens," having perhaps seen some of them green but none ripe.

The wild raspberry is by some there preferred to those that were transplanted thither from England, but I cannot be of their opinion.

Strawberries they have as delicious as any in the world and growing almost everywhere in the woods and fields. They are eaten almost by all creatures and yet are so plentiful that very few persons take care to transplant them but can find enough to fill their baskets when they have a mind in the deserted old fields.

There grow wild several sorts of good nuts, viz., chestnuts, chinquapins, hazelnuts, hickories, walnuts, etc.

Chestnuts are found upon very high trees, growing in barren ridges. They are something less than the French chestnut, but I think not differing at all in taste.

Chinquapins have a taste something like a chestnut and grow in a husk or burr, being of the same sort of substance but not so big as an acorn. They grow upon large bushes about as high as the common apple trees in England and either in the high or low, but always barren, ground.

Hazelnuts are there in infinite plenty in all the swamps and towards the heads of the rivers; whole acres of them are found upon the high land.

Hickory nuts are of several sorts, all growing upon great trees and in a husk like the French walnut, except that the husk is not so thick and more apt to open. Some of these nuts are enclosed in so hard a shell that a light hammer will hardly crack them; and when they are cracked their kernel is fastened with so firm a web that there's no coming at it. Several other sorts I have seen with thinner shells whose kernels may be got with less trouble. There are also several sorts of hickories called pig nuts, some of which have as thin a shell as the best French walnuts and yield their meat very easily.

They have a sort of walnut they call black walnuts which are as big again as any I ever saw in England but are very rank and oily, having a thick, hard, foul shell and come not clear of the husk as the walnut in France doth.

Grapes grow wild there in an incredible plenty and variety, some of which are very sweet and pleasant to the taste, others rough and harsh and perhaps fitter for wine or brandy. I have seen great trees covered with single vines, and those vines almost hid with the grapes. Of these wild grapes I have observed six very different kinds.

Two of these sorts grow among the sandbanks upon the edges of the low grounds and islands next the Bay and sea. They grow thin in small bunches and upon very low vines. These are noble grapes, and tho' they are wild in the woods are as large as the Dutch gooseberry. One species of them is white, the other purple, but both much alike in flavor.

A third kind is produced throughout the whole country in the swamps and sides of hills. These also grow upon small vines and in small bunches, but are themselves as big as the English bullace and of a rank taste when ripe, resembling the smell of a fox, from whence they are called fox grapes. All these three sorts when ripe make admirable tarts, being of a fleshy substance, and perhaps if rightly managed might make good raisins.

There are two species more that are common to the whole country, some of which are black and some blue on the outside, but are both red within. They grow upon vast large vines and bear very plentifully. The nice observer might perhaps distinguish them into several kinds, because they differ in color, size, and relish; but I shall divide them only into two, viz., the early and the late ripe. Of the former of these two sorts the French refugees at the Monacan town have lately made a sort of claret, tho' they were gathered off of the wild vines in the woods. I was told by a very good judge who tasted it that it was a pleasant, strong, and full bodied wine—from which we may conclude that if the wine was but tolerably good when made of the wild grape, which is shaded by the woods from the sun, it would be much better if produced of the same grape cultivated in a regular vineyard.

The sixth sort is far more palatable than the rest, and of the size of the white muscadine in England, but these are peculiar to the frontiers on the heads of the rivers. They grow upon very small vines which climb not higher than the shrub, or smallest bushes, on which they generally rest, or on the plants which annually spring out of the ground. But these are so greedily eaten by the small birds and other wild creatures to whom they hang convenient by the lowness of their vine that (as it was said of the Indian cherry) it is a great rarity to find any of them ripe, though they are in great plenty to be met with while they are green. These in all likelihood would make admirable wine, unless the earliness of their ripening may be an objection.

The year before the massacre, anno 1622, which destroyed so many good projects for Virginia, some French vignerons were sent thither to make an experiment of their vines. These people were so in love with the country that the character they then gave of it in their letters to the Company in England was very much to its advantage. Namely, that it far excelled their own country of Languedoc, the vines growing in great abundance and variety all over the land; that some of the grapes were of that unusual bigness that they did not believe them to be grapes until by opening them they had seen their kernels; that they had planted the cuttings of their vines at Michaelmas and had grapes from those very cuttings the spring following; adding, in the conclusion, that they had not heard of the like in any other country. Neither was this out of the way, for I have made the same experiment both of their natural vine and of the plants sent thither from England.

The honey and sugar trees are likewise spontaneous near the heads of the rivers. The honey tree bears a thick swelling pod full of honey, appearing at a distance like the bending pod of a bean or pea. The sugar tree yields a kind of sap or juice which by boiling is made into sugar. This juice is drawn out by wounding the trunk of the tree and placing a receiver under the wound. The

Indians make one pound of sugar out of eight pounds of liquor. Some of this sugar I examined very carefully. It was bright and moist with a large full grain, the sweetness of it being like that of good muscovada.

Though this discovery has not been made by the English above twelve or fourteen years, yet it has been known among the Indians longer than any now living can remember. It was found out by the English after this manner: The soldiers which were kept on the land frontiers to clear them of the Indians, taking their range through a piece of low ground about forty miles above the inhabited parts of Potomac River and resting themselves in the woods of those low grounds, observed an inspissate juice, like molasses, distilling from the tree. The heat of the sun had candied some of this juice, which gave the men a curiosity to taste it. They found it sweet, and by this process of nature learned to improve it into sugar. But these trees growing so far above the Christian inhabitants, it hath not yet been tried whether for quantity or quality it may be worthwhile to cultivate this discovery.

Thus the Canada Indians make sugar of the sap of a tree. And Peter Martyr mentions a tree that yields the like sap but without any description. The eleomeli of the ancients, a sweet juice like honey, is said to be got by wounding the olive tree. And the East Indians extract a sort of sugar they call jagra from the juice or potable liquor that flows from the coco tree. The whole process of boiling, graining, and refining of which is accurately set down by the authors of *Hortus Malabaricus.*

At the mouth of their rivers and all along upon the sea and Bay and near many of their creeks and swamps, grows the myrtle, bearing a berry of which they make a hard brittle wax of a curious green color which by refining becomes almost transparent. Of this they make candles which are never greasy to the touch nor melt with lying in the hottest weather. Neither does the snuff of these ever offend the smell, like that of a tallow candle; but instead of being disagreeable if an accident puts a candle out, it yields a pleasant fragrancy to all that are in the room, insomuch that nice people often put them out on purpose to have the incense of the expiring snuff.

The melting of these berries is said to have been first found out by a surgeon in New England who performed wonderful things with a salve made of them. This discovery is very modern, not-withstanding these countries have been so long settled.

The method of managing these berries is by boiling them in water till they come to be entirely dissolved, except the stone or seed in the middle which amounts in quantity to about half the bulk of the berry, the biggest of which is something less than a corn of pepper.

The cedar berries also have been experienced to yield the same sort of wax as the myrtle, their berries being as much larger than pepper as those of the myrtle are less.

There are also in the plains and rich grounds of the freshes abundance of hops which yield their product without any labor of the husbandman in weeding, hilling, or poling.

All over the country is interspersed here and there a surprising variety of curious plants and flowers. They have a sort of briar growing something like the sarsaparilla. The berry of this is as big as a pea and as round, being of a bright crimson color. It is very hard and finely polished by nature, so that it might be put to diverse ornamental uses.

There are several woods, plants, and earths which have been fit for the dying of curious colors. They have the puccoon and musquaspen, two roots with which the Indians use to paint them-selves red. There's the sumac and the sassafras, which make a deep yellow.

There's the rattlesnake root to which no remedy was ever yet found comparable, for it effectually cures the bite of a rattlesnake, which sometimes has been mortal in two minutes. If this medicine be early applied, it presently removes the infection and in two or three hours restores the patient to a perfect health, as if he had never been hurt. This operates by violent vomit and sweat.

The Jamestown weed [jimsonweed] (which resembles the thorny apple of Peru and I take to be the plant so called) is sup-posed to be one of the greatest coolers in the world. This, being an early plant, was gathered very young for a boiled salad by some of the soldiers sent thither to pacify the troubles of Bacon. And some of them eat plentifully of it, the effect of which was a very pleasant comedy, for they turned natural fools upon it for several days. One would blow up a feather in the air, another would dart straws at it with much fury, and another stark naked was sitting

up in a corner like a monkey grinning and making mows at them;
a fourth would fondly kiss and paw his companions and sneer in
their faces with a countenance more antic than any in a Dutch
droll. In this frantic condition they were confined, lest they should
in their folly destroy themselves, though it was observed that all
their actions were full of innocence and good nature. Indeed, they
were not very cleanly, for they would have wallowed in their own
excrements if they had not been prevented. A thousand such
simple tricks they played, and after eleven days returned to themselves again, not remembering anything that had passed.

Of spontaneous flowers they have an unknown variety—the
finest crown imperial in the world; the cardinal flower, so much
extolled for its scarlet color, is almost in every branch; the moccasin flower and a thousand others not yet known to English
herbalists. Almost all the year round, the levels and vales are beau-
tified with flowers of one kind or another, which make their woods
as fragrant as a garden. From these materials their wild bees make
vast quantities of honey, but their magazines are very often
rifled by bears, raccoons, and such like liquorish vermin.

About two years ago, walking out to take the air, I found a little
without my pasture fence a flower as big as a tulip and upon a
stalk resembling the stalk of a tulip. The flower was of a flesh
color, having a down upon one end, while the other was plain. The
form of it resembled the pudenda of a man and woman lovingly
joined in one. Not long after I had discovered this rarity and while
it was still in bloom, I drew a grave gentleman about a hundred
yards out of his way to see this curiosity, not telling him anything more than that it was a rarity and such perhaps as he had
never seen nor heard of. When we arrived at the place, I gathered
one of them and put it into his hand, which he had no sooner cast
his eye upon but he threw it away with indignation, as being
ashamed of this waggery of nature. It was impossible to persuade
him to touch it again or so much as to squint towards so immodest
a representation. Neither would I presume to mention such an in-
decency but that I thought it unpardonable to omit a production
so extraordinary.

There is also found the fine tulip-bearing laurel tree, which has
the pleasantest smell in the world and keeps blossoming and seed-
ing several months together. It delights much in gravelly branches

of crystal streams and perfumes the very woods with its odor; so also do the large tulip tree, which we call a poplar, the locust, which resembles much the jasmine, and the perfuming crabtree during their season. With one sort or other of these, as well as many other sweet flowering trees not named, the woods are almost everywhere adorned and yield a surprising variety to divert the traveler.

They find a world of medicinal plants likewise in that country, and amongst the rest the planters pretend to have a swamp root which infallibly cures all fevers and agues. The bark of the sassafras tree has been experimented to partake very much of the virtue of the *cortex peruviana*. The bark of the root of that which we call the prickly ash, being dried and powdered, has been found to be a specific in old ulcers and long-running sores. Infinite is the number of other valuable vegetables of every kind, but natural history not having been much my study, I am unwilling to do wrong to my subject by an unskillful description.

Several kinds of the creeping vines bearing fruit the Indians planted in their gardens or fields because they would have plenty of them always at hand; such as muskmelons, watermelons, pompions [pumpkins], cushaws, macocks, and gourds.

Their muskmelons resemble the large Italian kind and generally fill four or five quarts.

Their watermelons were much more large and of several kinds, distinguished by the color of their meat and seed: some are red, some yellow, and other white meated; and so of the seed—some are yellow, some red, and some black. But these are never of different colors in the same melon. They are excellently good and very pleasant to the taste as also to the eye, having the rind of a lively green color streaked and watered, the meat of a carnation, and the seed black and shining while it lies in the melon.

Their pompions I need not describe, but must say they are much larger and finer than any I ever heard of in England.

Their cushaws are a kind of pompion, of a bluish green color streaked with white when they are fit for use. They are larger than the pompions and have a long narrow neck.

Their macocks are a sort of melopepones or lesser sort of pompion. Of these they have great variety, but the Indian name macock serves for all—which name is still retained among them.

Yet the clypeatae are sometimes called cymnels (as are some others also), from the lenten cake of that name, which many of them very much resemble. Squash or squanter squash is their name among the northern Indians, and so they are called in New York and New England. These being boiled whole when the apple is young, and the shell tender and dished with cream or butter, relish very well with all sorts of butcher's meat, either fresh or salt. And whereas the pompion is never eaten till it be ripe, these are never eaten after they are ripe.

The Indians never eat the gourds but plant them for other uses. For when it is ripe the rind dries and grows as hard as the bark of a tree and the meat within is so consumed and dried away that there is then nothing left but the seed, which the Indians take clean out and afterwards use the shells instead of flagons and cups, as is done also in several other parts of the world.

The maracock, which is the fruit of what we call passion flower, our natives did not take the pains to plant, having enough of it growing everywhere, tho' they eat it with a great deal of pleasure. This fruit is about the size of a pullet's egg.

Besides all these, our natives had originally amongst them Indian corn, peas, beans, potatoes, and tobacco.

This Indian corn was the staff of food upon which the Indians did ever depend; for when sickness, bad weather, war, or any other ill accident kept them from hunting, fishing, and fowling, this, with the addition of some peas, beans, and such other fruits of the earth as were then in season, was the family's dependence and the support of their women and children.

There are four sorts of Indian corn, two of which are early ripe and two late ripe; all growing in the same manner. Every single grain of this when planted produces a tall upright stalk which has several ears hanging on the sides of it from six to ten inches long. Each ear is wrapped up in a cover of many folds to protect it from the injuries of the weather. In every one of these ears are several rows of grain set close to one another, with no other partition but of a very thin husk, so that oftentimes the increase of this grain amounts to above a thousand for one.

The two sorts which are early ripe are distinguished only by the size, which shows itself as well in the grain as in the ear and the stalk. There is some difference also in the time of ripening.

The lesser size of early ripe corn yields an ear not much larger than the handle of a case knife and grows upon a stalk between three and four foot high. Of this are commonly made two crops in a year, and perhaps there might be heat enough in England to ripen it.

The larger sort differs from the former only in largeness, the ear of this being seven or eight inches long, as thick as a child's leg, and growing upon a stalk nine or ten foot high. This is fit for eating about the latter end of May; whereas the smaller sort (generally speaking) affords ears fit to roast by the middle of May. The grains of both these sorts are as plump and swelled as if the skin were ready to burst.

The late ripe corn is diversified by the shape of the grain only, without any respect to the accidental differences in color—some being blue, some red, some yellow, some white, and some streaked. That therefore which makes the distinction is the plumpness or shriveling of the grain: the one looks as smooth and as full as the early ripe corn, and this they call flint corn; the other has a larger grain and looks shriveled with a dent on the back of the grain as if it had never come to perfection, and this they call she corn. This is esteemed by the planters as the best for increase and is universally chosen by them for planting, yet I can't see but that this also produces the flint corn accidentally among the other.

All these sorts are planted alike in rows, three, four, or five grains in a hill; the larger sort at four or five foot distance, the lesser sort nearer. The Indians used to give it one or two weedings and make a hill about it and so the labor was done. They likewise plant a bean in the same hill with the corn, upon whose stalk it sustains itself.

The Indians sowed peas sometimes in the intervals of the rows of corn, but more generally in a patch of ground by themselves. They have an unknown variety of them (but all of a kidney shape), some of which I have met with wild; but whence they had their Indian corn I can give no account, for I don't believe that it was spontaneous in those parts.

Their potatoes are either red or white, about as long as a boy's leg and sometimes as long and big as both the leg and thigh of a young child, and very much resembling it in shape. I take these kinds to be the same with those which are represented in the herbals to be Spanish potatoes. I am sure those called English or Irish potatoes are nothing like these either in shape, color, or taste. The way of propagating potatoes there is by cutting the small ones to pieces and planting the cuttings in hills of loose earth. But they are so tender that it is very difficult to preserve them in the winter, for the least frost coming at them rots and destroys them; and therefore people bury 'em under ground near the fire hearth all the winter until the time comes that their seedings are to be set.

How the Indians ordered their tobacco I am not certain, they now depending chiefly upon the English for what they smoke. But I am informed they used to let it all run to seed, only succoring the leaves to keep the sprouts from growing upon and starving them; and when it was ripe they pulled off the leaves, cured them in the sun, and laid them up for use. But the planters make a heavy bustle with it now and can't please the market neither.

5

Of the Fish

As for fish, both of fresh and salt water, of shellfish and others, no country can boast of more variety, greater plenty, or of better in their several kinds.

In the spring of the year, herrings come up in such abundance into their brooks and fords to spawn that it is almost impossible to ride through without treading on them. Thus do those poor creatures expose their own lives to some hazard out of their care to find a more convenient reception for their young, which are not yet alive. Thence it is that at this time of the year the freshes of the rivers, like that of the Broadruck, stink of fish.

Besides these herrings there come up likewise into the freshes from the sea multitudes of shads, rocks, sturgeon, and some few lampreys, which fasten themselves to the shad as the remora of imperatus is said to do to the shark of Tiburone. They continue their stay there about three months. The shads at their first coming up are fat and fleshy, but they waste so extremely in milting and spawning that at their going down they are poor and seem fuller of bones only because they have less flesh.

There is likewise great plenty of other fish all the summer long, and almost in every part of the rivers and brooks there are found of different kinds. Wherefore I shall not pretend to give a detail of them, but venture to mention the names only of such as I have eaten and seen myself and so leave the rest to those that are better skilled in natural history. However, I may add that besides all those that I have met with myself, I have heard of a great many very good sorts, both in the salts and freshes, and such people, too, as have not always spent their time in that country have commended them to me beyond any they had ever eat before.

Those which I know of myself I remember by the names of herrings, rocks, sturgeons, shads, alewives, sheep's heads, black and red drums, trouts, taylors, greenfish, sunfish, bass, chub, plaice, flounders, whitings, fatbacks, maids, wives, small turtle, crabs, oysters, mussels, cockles, shrimps, needlefish, bream, carp, pike, jack, mullets, eels, conger eels, perch, and cats, etc.

Those which I remember to have seen there of the kinds that are not eaten are the whale, porpoise, shark, dogfish, gar, stingray, thornback, sawfish, toadfish, frogfish, land crabs, fiddlers, and periwinkles.

Before the arrival of the English there, the Indians had fish in such vast plenty that the boys and girls would take a pointed stick and strike the lesser sort as they swam upon the flats. The larger fish that kept in deeper water they were put to a little more difficulty to take. But for these they made weirs—that is, a hedge of small rived sticks or reeds of the thickness of a man's finger. These they wove together in a row with straps of green oak or other tough woods, so close that the small fish could not pass through. Upon high-water mark they pitched one end of this hedge, and the other they extended into the river to the depth of eight or ten feet, fastening it with stakes, making cods [bags, pouches] out from the hedge on one side almost at the end, and leaving a gap for the fish to go into them; which they contrived so that the fish could easily find their passage into those cods when they were at the gap but not see their way out again when they were in. Thus if they offered to pass through they were taken.

Sometimes they made such a hedge as this quite across a creek at high water, and at low would go into the run, so contracted into a narrow compass, and take out what fish they pleased.

At the falls of the rivers, where the water is shallow and the current strong, the Indians use another kind of weir, thus made: They make a dam of loose stone, whereof there is plenty at hand, quite across the river, leaving one, two, or more spaces or trunnels for the water to pass thro'; at the mouth of which they set a pot of reeds wove in form of a cone, whose base is about three foot and perpendicular ten, into which the swiftness of the current carries the fish and wedges them so fast they cannot possibly return.

The Indian way of catching sturgeon when they came into the narrow part of the rivers was by a man's clapping a noose over their tail and by keeping fast his hold. Thus a fish finding itself entangled would flounce and often pull him under water, and then that man was counted a cockarouse, or brave fellow, that would not let go till with swimming, wading, and diving he had tired the sturgeon and brought it ashore. These sturgeons would also often leap into their canoes in crossing the river, as many of them do still every year into the boats of the English.

They have also another way of fishing like those on the Euxine Sea, by the help of a blazing fire by night. They make a hearth in the middle of their canoe, raising it within two inches of the edge; upon this they lay their burning light wood, split into small shivers, each splinter whereof will blaze and burn end for end like a candle. 'Tis one man's work to tend this fire and keep it flaming. At each end of the canoe stands an Indian with a gig or pointed spear, setting the canoe forward with the butt end of the spear as gently as he can, by that means stealing upon the fish without any noise or disturbing of the water. Then they with great dexterity dart these spears into the fish and so take 'em. Now there is a double convenience in the blaze of this fire, for it not only dazzles the eyes of the fish, which will lie still glaring upon it, but like-wise discovers the bottom of the river clearly to the fisherman, which the daylight does not.

'Tis a good diversion to observe the manner of the fishing hawks preying upon fish, which may be seen every fair day all the summer long, especially in a morning. At the first coming of the fish in the spring, these birds of prey are surprisingly eager. I believe in the dead of winter they fish farther off at sea or remain among the craggy uninhabited islands upon the seacoast. I have often been pleasantly entertained by seeing these hawks take the fish out of the water, and as they were flying away with their quarry, the bald eagles take it from them again. I have often observed the first of these hover over the water and rest upon the wing some minutes together without the least change of place, and then from a vast height dart directly into the water and there plunge down to the space of half a minute or more and at last bring up with him a fish which he could hardly rise with; then, having got upon the wing again, he would shake himself so powerfully that he threw the water like a mist about him. Afterwards, away he'd fly to the woods with his game, if he were not overlooked by the bald eagle and robbed by the way, which very frequently happens. For the bald eagle no sooner perceives a hawk that has taken his prey, but he immediately pursues and strives to get above him in the air, which if he can once attain, the hawk for fear of being torn by him lets the fish drop and so by the loss of his dinner compounds for his own safety. The poor fish is no sooner loosed from the hawk's talons but the eagle shoots himself with wonderful swiftness after it and catches it in the air, leaving all further pursuit of the hawk, which has no other remedy but to go and fish for another.

Walking once with a gentleman in an orchard by the riverside —early in the spring before the fish were by us perceived to appear in shoal water or near the shores, and before any had been caught by the people—we heard a great noise in the air just over our heads, and looking up we see an eagle in close pursuit of a hawk that had a great fish in his pounces. The hawk was as low as the apple trees before he would let go his fish, thinking to recover the wood which was just by, where the eagles never dare follow for fear of bruising themselves. But notwithstanding, the fish was dropped so low, and tho' it did not fall above thirty yards from us, yet we with our hollowing, running, and casting up our hats could hardly save the fish from the eagle; and if it had been dropped two yards higher he would have got it. But we at last took possession of it alive, carried it home, and had it dressed forthwith. It served five of us very plentifully without any other addition and some to the servants. This fish was a rock near two foot long, very fat, and a great rarity for the time of year as well as for the manner of its being taken.

These fishing hawks in more plentiful seasons will catch a fish and loiter about with it in the air on purpose to have a chase with an eagle, and when he does not appear soon enough the hawk will make a saucy noise and insolently defy him. This has been frequently seen by persons who have observed their fishings.

6

Of Wild Fowl and Hunted Game

As in summer the rivers and creeks are filled with fish, so in winter they are in many places covered with fowl. There are such a multitude of swans, geese, brants, sheldrakes, ducks of several sorts, mallard, teal, bluewings, and many other kinds of waterfowl, that the plenty of them is incredible. I am but a small sportsman, yet with a fowling piece have killed above twenty of them at a shot. In like manner are the millponds and great runs in the woods stored with these wild fowl at certain seasons of the year.

The shores, marshy grounds, swamps, and savannas are also stored with the like plenty of other game of all sorts, as cranes, curlews, herons, snipes, woodcocks, saurers, oxeyes, plover, larks, and many other good birds for the table that they have not yet found a name for. Not to mention beavers, otters, muskrats, minxes, and an infinite number of other wild creatures.

Altho' the inner lands want these benefits (which, however, no pond or slash is without), yet even they have the advantage of wild turkeys of an incredible bigness, pheasants, partridges, pigeons, and an infinity of small birds as well as deer, hares, foxes, raccoons, squirrels, possums. And upon the frontier plantations they meet with bears, panthers, wildcats, elks, buffaloes, and wild hogs which yield pleasure as well as profit to the sportsman. And tho' some of these names may seem frightful to the English, who hear not of them in their own country, yet they are not so there. For all these creatures ever fly from the face of man, doing no damage but to the cattle and hogs, which the Indians never troubled themselves about.

Here I can't omit a strange rarity in the female possum, which I myself have seen. They have a false belly, or loose skin quite over the belly. This never sticks to the flesh of the belly but may be looked into at all times after they have been concerned in procreation. In the hinder part of this is an overture big enough for a small hand to pass into. Hither the young ones, after they are full-haired and strong enough to run about, do fly whenever any danger appears or when they go to rest or suck. This they continue till they have learned to live without the dam. But what is yet stranger, the young ones are bred in this false belly without ever being within the true one. They are formed at the teat, and there they grow for several weeks together into perfect shape, becoming visibly larger till at last they get strength, sight, and hair, and then they drop off and rest in this false belly, going in and out at pleasure. I have observed them thus fastened at the teat from the bigness of a fly until they became as large as a mouse. Neither is it any hurt to the old one to open this budget and look in upon her young.

The Indians had no other way of taking their water or land fowl but by the help of bows and arrows; yet so great was their plenty that with this weapon only they killed what numbers they pleased. And when the waterfowl kept far from shore (as in warmer weather they sometimes did) they took their canoes and paddled after them.

But they had a better way of killing the elks, buffaloes, deer, and greater game—by a method which we call fire hunting. That is, a company of them would go together into the woods at any time in the winter when the leaves were fallen and so dry that they would burn. And being come to the place designed, they would fire the woods in a circle of five or six miles compass, and when they had completed the first round they retreated inward, each at his due distance, and put fire to the leaves and grass afresh to accelerate the work, which ought to be finished with the day. This they repeat till the circle be so contracted that they can see their game herded all together in the middle, panting and almost stifled with heat and smoke; for the poor creatures being frightened at the flame keep running continually round thinking to run from it, and dare not pass through the fire; by which means they are brought at last into a very narrow compass. Then the Indians let fly their arrows at them and (which is very strange) tho' they stand all round quite clouded in smoke, yet they rarely shoot each other. By this means they destroy all the beasts collected within that circle. They make all this slaughter only for the sake of the skins, leaving the carcasses to perish in the woods.

The Indians have many pretty inventions to discover and come up to the deer, turkeys, and other game undiscerned; but that being an art known to very few English there, I will not be so accessary to the destruction of their game as to make it public. I shall therefore only tell you that when they go a-hunting into the outlands they commonly go out for the whole season with their wives and family. At the place where they find the most game they build up a convenient number of small cabins, wherein they live during that season. These cabins are both begun and finished in two or three days, and after the season is over they make no further account of them.

This and a great deal more was the natural production of that country which the native Indians enjoyed without the course of industry, their diversion alone and not their labor supplying their necessities. The women and children indeed were so far provident as to lay up some of the nuts and fruits of the earth in their season for their further occasions. But none of the toils of husbandry were exercised by this happy people, except the bare planting a little corn and melons which took up only a few days in the summer, the rest being wholly spent in the pursuit of their pleasures. And indeed all that the English have done since their going thither has been only to make some of these native pleasures more scarce by an inordinate and unseasonable use of them, hardly making improvements equivalent to that damage.

I shall in the next book give an account of the Indians themselves, their religion, laws, and customs; that so both the country and its primitive inhabitants may be considered together in that original state of nature in which the English found them. Afterwards I will treat of the present state of the English there and the alterations—I can't call them improvements—they have made at this day.

BOOK THREE

Of the Indians, Their Religion, Laws, and Customs in War and Peace

1

Of the Persons of the Indians and Their Dress

The Indians are of the middling and largest stature of the English. They are straight and well proportioned, having the cleanest and most exact limbs in the world. They are so perfect in their outward frame that I never heard of one single Indian that was either dwarfish, crooked, bandy-legged, or otherwise misshapen. But if they have any such practice among them, as the Romans had, of exposing such children till they died as were weak and misshapen at their birth, they are very shy of confessing it, and I could never yet learn that they had.

Their color when they are grown up is a chestnut brown and tawny, but much clearer in their infancy. Their skin comes afterwards to harden and grow blacker by greasing and sunning themselves. They have generally coal black hair and very black eyes which are most commonly graced with that sort of squint which many of the Jews are observed to have. Their women are generally beautiful, possessing an uncommon delicacy of shape and features and wanting no charm but that of a fair complexion.

The men wear their hair cut after several fanciful fashions, sometimes greased and sometimes painted. The great men, or better sort, preserve a long lock behind for distinction. They pull their beards up by the roots with a mussel shell, and both men and women do the same by the other parts of their body for cleanliness' sake. The women wear the hair of the head very long, either hanging at their backs or brought before in a single lock bound up with a fillet of peak or beads; sometimes also they wear it neatly tied up in a knot behind. It is commonly greased and shining black, but never painted.

The people of condition of both sexes wear a sort of coronet on their heads from four to six inches broad, open at the top, and composed of peak or beads, or else of both interwoven together and worked into figures made by a nice mixture of the colors. Sometimes they wear a wreath of dyed furs, as likewise bracelets, on their necks and arms. The common people go bareheaded, only sticking large shining feathers about their heads as their fancies lead them.

Their clothes are a large mantle carelessly wrapped about their bodies and sometimes girt close in the middle with a girdle. The upper part of this mantle is drawn close upon the shoulders, and the other hangs below their knees. When that's thrown off, they have only for modesty sake a piece of cloth or a small skin tied round their waist which reaches down to the middle of the thigh. The common sort tie only a string around their middle and pass a piece of cloth or skin around between their thighs which they turn at each end over the string.

Their shoes, when they wear any, are made of an entire piece of buckskin, except when they sew a piece to the bottom to thicken the sole. They are fastened on with running strings, the skin being drawn together like a purse on the top of the foot and tied round the ankle. The Indian name of this kind of shoe is moccasin.

I don't find that the Indians have any other distinction in their dress or the fashion of their hair than only what a greater degree of riches enables them to make; except it be their religious persons, who are known by the particular cut of the hair and the unusual figure of their garments, as our clergy are distinguished by their canonical habit.

The habit of the Indian priest is a cloak made in the form of a woman's petticoat; but instead of tying it about their middle they fasten the gatherings about their neck and tie it upon the right shoulder, always keeping one arm out to use upon occasion. This cloak hangs even at the bottom but reaches no lower than the middle of the thigh; but what is most particular in it is that it is constantly made of a skin dressed soft, with the pelt or fur on the outside and reversed; insomuch that when the cloak has been a little worn, the hair falls down in flakes and looks very shagged and frightful.

The cut of their hair is likewise peculiar to their function, for 'tis all shaven close except a thin crest like a cockscomb which stands bristling up and runs in a semi-circle from the forehead up along the crown to the nape of the neck. They likewise have a border of hair over the forehead which by its own natural strength and by the stiffening it receives from grease and paint will stand out like the peak of a bonnet.

The dress of the women is little different from that of the men, except in the tying of their hair. The ladies of distinction wear deep necklaces, pendants, and bracelets made of small cylinders of the conch shell, which they call peak. They likewise keep their skin clean and shining with oil, while the men are commonly bedaubed all over with paint.

They are remarkable for having small round breasts and so firm that they are hardly ever observed to hang down, even in old women. They commonly go naked as far as the navel downward, and upward to the middle of the thigh, by which means they have the advantage of discovering their fine limbs and complete shape.

2

Of the Marriages Amongst the Indians and Management of Their Children

The Indians have their solemnities of marriage and esteem the vows made at that time as most sacred and inviolable. Notwithstanding, they allow both the man and the wife to part upon disagreement; yet so great is the disreputation of a divorce that married people, to avoid the character of inconstant and ungenerous, very rarely let their quarrels proceed to a separation. However, when it does so happen they reckon all the ties of matrimony dissolved, and each hath the liberty of marrying another. But infidelity is accounted the most unpardonable of all crimes in either of the parties as long as the contract continues.

In these separations the children go, according to the affection of the parent, with the one or the other, for children are not reckoned a charge among them, but rather riches, according to the blessing of the Old Testament. And if they happen to differ about dividing their children, their method is then to part them equally, allowing the man the first choice.

Tho' the young Indian women are said to prostitute their bodies for wampum peak, runtees, beads, and other such like fineries, yet I never could find any ground for the accusation and believe it only to be an unjust scandal upon them. This I know, that if ever they have a child while they are single it is such a disgrace to them that they never after get husbands. Besides, I must do 'em the justice to say I never heard of a child any of them had before marriage, and the Indians themselves disown any such custom, tho' they acknowledge at the same time that the maidens are entirely at their own disposal and may manage their persons as they think fit.

Indeed, I believe this story to be an aspersion cast on those innocent creatures by reason of the freedom they take in conversation which uncharitable Christians interpret as criminal, upon no other ground than the guilt of their own consciences.

The Indian damsels are full of spirit and from thence are always inspired with mirth and good humor. They are extremely given to laugh, which they do with a grace not to be resisted. The excess of life and fire which they never fail to have makes them frolicsome but without any real imputation to their innocence. However, this is ground enough for the English, who are not very nice in distinguishing betwixt guilt and harmless freedom to think them incontinent. Tho' it be with as little justice as the jealous Spaniards condemn the liberty used by the women of France, which are much more chaste than their own ladies which they keep under the strictest confinement.

The manner of the Indians treating their young children is very strange, for instead of keeping them warm at their first entry into the world and wrapping them up with I don't know how many cloths, according to our fond custom, the first thing they do is to dip the child over head and ears in cold water and then to bind it naked to a convenient board, having a hole fitly placed for evacuation; but they always put cotton, wool, fur, or other soft thing for the body to rest easy on between the child and the board.

In this posture they keep it several months, till the bones begin to harden, the joints to knit, and the limbs to grow strong; and then they let it loose from the board, suffering it to crawl about, except when they are feeding or playing with it.

While the child is thus at the board, they either lay it flat on its back or set it leaning on one end, or else hang it up by a string fastened to the upper end of the board for that purpose, the child and board being all this while carried about together. As our women undress their children to clean them and shift their linen, so they do theirs to wash and grease them.

The method the women have of carrying their children after they are suffered to crawl about is very particular: they carry them at their backs in summer, taking one leg of the child under their arm and the counter arm of the child in their hand over their shoulder, the other leg hanging down, and the child all the while holding fast with its other hand; but in winter they carry them in the hollow of their matchcoat at their back, leaving nothing but the child's head out.

3

Of the Towns, Buildings, and Fortifications of the Indians

The method of the Indian settlements is altogether by cohabitation in townships from fifty to five hundred families in a town, and each of these towns is commonly a kingdom. Sometimes one king has the command of several of these towns when they happen to be united in his hands by descent or conquest. But in such cases there is always a viceregent appointed in the dependent town who is at once governor, judge, chancellor, and has the same power and authority which the king himself has in the town where he resides. This viceroy is obligated to pay to his principal some small tribute as an acknowledgement of his submission, as likewise to follow him to his wars whenever he is required.

The manner the Indians have of building their houses is very slight and cheap. When they would erect a wigwam, which is the Indian name for a house, they stick saplings into the ground by one end and bend the other at the top, fastening them together by strings made of fibrous roots, the rind of trees, or of the green wood of the white oak, which will rive into thongs. The smallest sort of these cabins are conical like a beehive, but the larger are built in an oblong form, and both are covered with the bark of trees which will rive off into great flakes. Their windows are little holes left open for the passage of the light, which in bad weather they stop with shutters of the same bark, opening the leeward windows for air and light. Their chimney, as among the true-born Irish, is a little hole in the top of the house to let out the smoke, having no sort of funnel or anything within to confine the smoke from ranging through the whole roof of the cabins if the vent will not let it out fast enough. The fire is always made in the middle of the cabin. Their door is a pendent mat when they are home, but when they go abroad they barricado it with great logs of wood set against the mat, which are sufficient to keep out wild beasts. There's never more than one room in a house, except in some houses of state or religion where the partition is made only by mats and loose poles.

Their houses, or cabins as we call them, are by this ill method of building continually smoky when they have fire in them; but to ease that inconvenience and to make the smoke less troublesome to their eyes, they generally burn pine or lightwood (that is, the fat knots of dead pine), the smoke of which does not offend the eyes but smuts the skin exceedingly and is perhaps another occasion of the darkness of their complexion.

Their seats, like those in the eastern part of the world, are the ground itself, and as the people of distinction amongst them used carpets, so cleanliness has taught the better sort of these to spread matchcoats and mats to sit on.

They take up their lodging in the sides of their cabins upon a couch made of board, sticks, or reeds which are raised from the ground upon forks and covered with mats or skins. Sometimes they lie upon a bearskin or other thick pelt, dressed with the hair on and laid upon the ground near a fire, covering themselves with their matchcoats. In warm weather a single mat is their only bed, and another rolled up their pillow. In their travels a grass plat under the covert of a shady tree is all the lodgings they require and is as pleasant and refreshing to them as a down bed and fine holland sheets are to us.

Their fortifications consist only of a palisado of about ten or twelve foot high, and when they would make themselves very safe they treble the pale. They often encompass their whole town, but for the most part only their kings' houses, and as many others as they judge sufficient to harbor all their people when an enemy comes against them. They never fail to secure within their palisado all their religious relics and the remains of their princes. Within this enclosure they likewise take care to have a supply of water and to make a place for a fire, which they frequently dance round with great solemnity.

4

Of Their Cookery and Food

Their cookery has nothing commendable in it but that it is performed with little trouble. They have no other sauce but a good stomach, which they seldom want. They boil, broil, or toast all the meat they eat, and it is very common with them to boil fish as well as flesh with their hominy. This is Indian corn soaked, broken in a mortar, husked, and then boiled in water over a gentle fire for ten or twelve hours to the consistence of furmity. The thin of this is what my Lord Bacon calls cream of maize and highly commends for an excellent sort of nutriment.

They have two ways of broiling; viz., one by laying the meat itself upon the coals, the other by laying it upon sticks raised upon forks at some distance above the live coals, which heats more gently and dries up the gravy. This they, and we also from them, call barbecuing.

They skin and paunch all sorts of quadrupeds. They draw and pluck their fowl, but their fish they dress with their scales on without gutting; but in eating they leave the scales, entrails, and bones to be thrown away.

They never serve up different sorts of victuals in one dish—as roast and boiled, fish and flesh—but always serve them up in several vessels.

They bake their bread either in cakes before the fire or in loaves on a warm hearth, covering the loaf first with leaves, then with warm ashes, and afterwards with coals over all.

Their food is fish and flesh of all sorts and that which participates of both, as the beaver, a small kind of turtle or terrapins (as we call them), and several species of snakes. They likewise eat grubs, the nymphae of wasps, some kinds of scarabaei, cicadae, etc. These last are such as are sold in the markets of Fez, and such as the Arabians, Lybians, Parthians, and Ethiopians commonly eat; so that these are not a new diet, tho' a very slender one; and we are informed that St. John was dieted upon locusts and wild honey.

They make an excellent broth of the head and umbles of a deer, which they put into the pot all bloody. This seems to resemble the *jus nigrum* of the Spartans, made with the blood and bowels of a hare. They eat not the brains with the head, but dry and reserve them to dress their leather with.

They eat all sorts of peas, beans, and other pulse, both parched and boiled. They make their bread of the Indian corn, wild oats, or the seed of the sunflower. But when they eat their bread, they eat it alone and not with their meat.

They have no salt among them but for seasoning use the ashes of hickory, stickweed, or some other wood or plant affording a salt ash.

They delight much to feed on roasting ears; that is, the Indian corn gathered green and milky before it is grown to its full bigness and roasted before the fire in the ear. For the sake of this diet, which they love exceedingly, they are very careful to procure all the several sorts of Indian corn before mentioned, by which means they contrive to prolong their season. And indeed this is a very sweet and pleasing food.

They accustom themselves to no set meals, but eat night and day when they have plenty of provisions or if they have got anything that is a rarity. They are very patient of hunger when by any accident they happen to have nothing to eat, which they make more easy to them by girding up their bellies, just as the wild Arabs are said to do in their long marches; by which means they are less sensible of the impressions of hunger.

Among all this variety of food, nature hath not taught them

the use of any other drink than water, which tho' they have in cool and pleasant springs everywhere, yet they will not drink that if they can get pond water, or such as has been warmed by the sun and weather. Baron LaHontan tells of a sweet juice of maple which the Indians to the northward gave him, mingled with water; but our Indians use no such drink. For their strong drink they are altogether beholding to us and are so greedy of it that most of them will be drunk as often as they find an opportunity. Notwithstanding which it is a prevailing humor among them not to taste any strong drink at all unless they can get enough to make them quite drunk, and then they go as solemnly about it as if it were part of their religion.

The spoons which they eat with do generally hold half a pint, and they laugh at the English for using small ones which they must be forced to carry so often to their mouths that their arms are in danger of being tired before their belly.

5

Of the Traveling, Reception, and Entertainment of the Indians

Their travels they perform altogether on foot, the fatigue of which they endure to admiration. They make no other provision for their journey but their gun and bow to supply them with food for many hundred miles together. If they carry any flesh in their marches they barbecue it, or rather dry it by degrees, at some distance over the clear coals of a wood fire. Their sauce to this dry meat (if they have any besides a good stomach) is only a little bear's oil or oil of acorns, which last they force out by boiling the acorns in a strong lye. Sometimes also in their travels each man takes with him a pint or quart of rockahominy, that is, the finest Indian corn, parched and beaten to powder. When they find their stomach empty (and cannot stay for the tedious cookery of other things), they put about a spoonful of this into their mouths and drink a draught of water upon it, which stays their stomachs and enables them to pursue their journey without delay. But their main dependence is upon the game they kill by the way, and the natural fruits of the earth. They take no care about lodging in these journeys, but content themselves with the shade of a tree or a little high grass.

When they fear being discovered or followed by an enemy in their marches, they every morning (having first agreed where they shall rendezvous at night) disperse themselves into the woods and each takes a several way that so the grass or leaves being but singly pressed may rise again and not betray them. For the Indians are very artful in following a track, even where the impressions are not visible to other people, especially if they have any advantage from the looseness of the earth, from the stiffness of the grass, or the stirring of the leaves which in the winter season lie very thick upon the ground; and likewise afterwards, if they do not happen to be burned.

When in their travels they meet with any waters which are not fordable, they make canoes of birch bark by slipping it whole off the tree in this manner: First, they gash the bark quite round the tree at the length they would have the canoe of, then slit down the length from end to end. When that is done, they with their tomahawks easily open the bark and strip it whole off. Then they force it open with sticks in the middle, slope the underside of the ends, and sew them up, which helps to keep the belly open. Or if the birch trees happen to be small, they sew the bark of two together. The seams they daub with clay or mud and then pass over in these canoes by two or three or more at a time, according as they are in bigness. By reason of the lightness of these boats they can easily carry them overland if they foresee that they are like to meet with any more waters that may impede their march; or else they leave them at the waterside, making no farther account of them except it be to repass the same waters in their return.

They have a peculiar way of receiving strangers and distinguishing whether they come as friends or enemies, tho' they do not understand each other's language, and that is by a singular method of smoking tobacco, in which these things are always observed:

1. They take a pipe much larger and bigger than the common tobacco pipe, expressly made for that purpose, with which all

towns are plentifully provided. They call them the Pipes of Peace.

2. This pipe they always fill with tobacco before the face of the strangers and light it.

3. The chief man of the Indians to whom the strangers come takes two or three whiffs and then hands it to the chief of the strangers.

4. If the stranger refuses to smoke in it, 'tis a sign of war.

5. If it be peace, the chief of the strangers takes a whiff or two in the pipe and presents it to the next great man of the town they come to visit. He, after taking two or three whiffs, gives it back to the next of the strangers, and so on alternately, until they have passed all the persons of note on each side, and then the ceremony is ended.

They have a remarkable way of entertaining all strangers of condition, which is performed after the following manner: First, the king or queen with a guard and a great retinue, march out of the town a quarter or half a mile and carry mats for their accommodation. When they meet the strangers they invite them to sit down upon those mats. Then they pass the ceremony of the pipe, and afterwards, having spent about half an hour in grave discourse, they get up all together and march into the town. Here the first compliment is to wash the courteous traveler's feet, then he is treated at a sumptuous entertainment served up by a great number of attendants. After which he is diverted with antic Indian dances performed both by men and women and accompanied with great variety of wild music. At this rate he is regaled till bedtime, when a brace of young beautiful virgins are chosen to wait upon him that night for his particular refreshment. These damsels are to undress this happy gentleman, and as soon as he is in bed they gently lay themselves down by him, one on one side of him and the other on the other. They esteem it a breach of hospitality not to submit to everything he desires of them. This kind of ceremony is used only to men of great distinction. And the young women are so far from suffering in their reputation for this civility that they are envied for it by all the other girls as having had the greatest honor done them in the world.

After this manner perhaps many of the heroes were begotten in old time who boasted themselves to be the sons of some wayfaring god.

6

Of the Learning and Languages
of the Indians

These Indians have no sort of letters to express their words by, but when they would communicate anything that cannot be delivered by message they do it by a sort of hieroglyphic or representation of birds, beasts, or other things, showing their different meaning by the various forms described and by the different positions of the figures.

The Indians when they travel never so small a way, being much embroiled in war one with another, use several marks painted upon their shoulders to distinguish themselves by and show what nation they are of. The usual mark is one, two, or three arrows. One nation paints these arrows upwards, another downwards, a third sideways, and others again use other distinctions.

Their language differs very much as anciently in the several parts of Britain, so that nations at a moderate distance do not understand one another. However, they have a sort of general language like what LaHontan calls the Algonquin, which is understood by the chief men of many nations, as Latin is in most parts of Europe and lingua franca quite through the Levant.

The general language here used is said to be that of the Occaneeches, tho' they have been but a small nation ever since those parts were known to the English. But in what this language may differ from that of the Algonquins I am not able to determine.

7

Of the War and Peace
of the Indians

When they are about to undertake any war or other solemn enterprise the king summons a convention of his great men to assist at a grand council, which in their language is called a matchacomoco. At these assemblies 'tis the custom, especially when a war is expected, for the young men to paint themselves irregularly with black, red, white, and several other motley colors, making one half of their face red (for instance) and the other half black or white with great circles of a different hue round their eyes; with monstrous mustachoes and a thousand fantastical figures all over the rest of their body. And to make themselves appear yet more ugly and frightful, they strow feathers, down, or the hair of beasts upon the paint while it is still moist and capable of making those light substances stick fast on. When they are thus formidably equipped, they rush into the matchacomoco and instantly begin some very grotesque dance, holding their arrows or tomahawks in their hands and all the while singing the ancient glories of their nation and especially of their own families, threatening and making signs with their tomahawk what a dreadful havoc they intend to make amongst their enemies.

Notwithstanding these terrible airs they give themselves, they are very timorous when they come to action and rarely perform any open or bold feats; but the execution they do is chiefly by surprise and ambuscade.

The fearfulness of their nature makes 'em very jealous and implacable. Hence it is that when they get a victory they destroy man, woman, and child to prevent all future resentments.

I can't think it anything but their jealousy that makes them exclude the lineal issue from succeeding immediately to the crown. Thus if a king have several legitimate children, the crown does not descend in a direct line to his children but to his brother by the same mother, if he have any, and for want of such to the children of his eldest sister, always respecting the descent by the female as the surer side. But the crown goes to the male heir (if any be) in equal degree, and for want of such to the female preferably to any male that is more distant.

As in the beginning of a war they have assemblies for consultation, so upon any victory or other great success they have public meetings again for processions and triumphs. I never saw one of these but have heard that they are accompanied with all the marks of a wild and extravagant joy.

They use formal embassies for treating and very ceremonious ways in concluding of peace or else some other memorable action such as burying a tomahawk and raising a heap of stones thereon,

as the Hebrews did over Absalom, or of planting a tree in token
that all enmity is buried with the tomahawk, that all the desola-
tions of war are at an end, and that friendship shall flourish among
them like a tree.

8

Concerning the Religion and Worship of the Indians

I have been at several of the Indian towns and conversed with
some of the most sensible of them in that country, but I could
learn little from them, it being reckoned sacrilege to divulge the
principles of their religion. However, the following adventure discovered something of it: As I was ranging the woods with some
other friends, we fell upon their quioccasan (which is their house
of religious worship) at a time when the whole town were gathered
together in another place to consult about the bounds of the land
given them by the English.

Thus finding ourselves masters of so fair an opportunity (because we knew the Indians were engaged) we resolved to make
use of it and to examine their quioccasan, the inside of which they
never suffer any Englishman to see. And having removed about
fourteen logs from the door with which it was barricadoed, we
went in and at first found nothing but naked walls and a fireplace
in the middle. This house was about eighteen foot wide and thirty
foot long, built after the manner of their other cabins but larger,
with a hole in the middle of the roof to vent the smoke, the door
being at one end. Round about the house at some distance from
it were set up posts with faces carved on them and painted. We
did not observe any window or passage for the light except the
door and the vent of the chimney. At last we observed that at the
farther end about ten foot of the room was cut off by a partition
of very close mats, and it was dismal dark behind that partition.
We were at first scrupulous to enter this obscure place, but at last
we ventured, and groping about we felt some posts in the middle.
Then reaching our hands up those posts we found large shelves,
and upon these shelves three mats, each of which was rolled up

and sewed fast. These we handed down to the light, and to save time in unlacing the seams we made use of a knife and ripped them without doing any damage to the mats. In one of these we found some vast bones which we judged to be the bones of men. Particularly we measured one thighbone and found it two foot nine inches long. In another mat we found some Indian tomahawks finely graved and painted. Among these tomahawks was the largest that ever I saw. There was fastened to it a wild turkey's beard painted red, and two of the longest feathers of his wings hung dangling at it by a string of about six inches long tied to the end of the tomahawk. In the third mat there was something which we took to be their idol, tho' of an underling sort and wanted putting together. The pieces were these: First, a board three foot and a half long with one indenture at the upper end like a fork to fasten the head upon; from thence half way down were half hoops nailed to the edges of the board at about four inches distance, which were bowed out to represent the breast and belly; on the lower half was another board of half the length of the other, fastened to it by joints or pieces of wood which being set on each side stood out about fourteen inches from the body and half as high. We supposed the use of these to be for the bowing out of the knees when the image was set up. There were packed up with these things red and blue pieces of cotton cloth and rolls made up for arms, thighs, and legs bent to at the knees. It would be difficult to see one of these images at this day because the Indians are extreme shy of exposing them. We put the cloths upon the hoops for the body and fastened on the arms and legs to have a view of the representation, but the head and rich bracelets which it is usually adorned with were not there or at least we did not find them. We had not leisure to make a very narrow search, for having spent about an hour in this inquiry we feared the business of the Indians might be near over, and that if we stayed longer we might be caught offering an affront to their superstition. For this reason we wrapped up these holy materials in their several mats again and laid them on the shelf where we found them. This image when dressed up might look very venerable in that dark place where 'tis not possible to see it but by the glimmering light that is let in by lifting up a piece of the matting, which we observed to be conveniently hung for that purpose. For when the light of the door and chimney glance in several directions upon the image thro' that little passage, it must needs make a strange representation which those poor people are taught to worship with a devout ignorance. There are other things that contribute towards carrying on this imposture: First, the chief conjurer enters within the partition in the dark and may undiscerned move the image as he pleases; secondly, a priest of authority stands in the room with the people to keep them from being too inquisitive, under the penalty of the deity's displeasure and his own censure.

Their idol bears a several name in every nation—as Okee, Quioccos, Kiwasa. They do not look upon it as one single being but reckon there are many of them of the same nature. They likewise believe that there are tutelar deities in every town.

Once in my travels in very cold weather I met at an Englishman's house with an Indian of whom an extraordinary character had been given me for his ingenuity and understanding. When I see he had no other Indian with him, I thought I might be the more free, and therefore I made much of him—seating him close by a large fire, and giving him plenty of strong cider which I hoped would make him good company and openhearted. After I found him well warmed (for unless they be surprised some way or other they will not talk freely of their religion) I asked him concerning their God and what their notions of him were? He freely told me they believed God was universally beneficent, that his dwelling was in the heavens above, and that the influences of his goodness reached to the earth beneath; that he was incomprehensible in his excellence and enjoyed all possible felicity, that his duration was eternal, his perfection boundless, and that he possesses everlasting indolence and ease. I told him I had heard that they worshiped the devil and asked why they did not rather worship God whom they had so high an opinion of and who would give them all good things and protect them from any mischief that the devil could do them? To this his answer was that 'tis true God is the giver of all good things, but they flow naturally and promiscuously from him; that they are showered down upon all men indifferently without distinction; that God does not trouble himself with the impertinent affairs of men, nor is concerned at what they do, but leaves them to make the most of their free will and to secure as many as they can of the good things that flow from him. That therefore it was to no purpose either to fear or worship him; but on the contrary if they did not pacify the evil spirit and make him propitious, he would take away or spoil all those good things that God had given and ruin their health, their peace, and their plenty by sending war, plague, and famine among them. For, said he, this evil spirit is always busying himself with our affairs and frequently visiting us, being present in the air, in the thunder, and in the storms. He told me farther that he expected adoration and sacrifice from them on pain of his displeasure, and that therefore they thought it convenient to make their court to him. I then asked him concerning the image which they worship in their quioccasan and assured him that it was a dead, insensible log equipped with a bundle of clouts, a mere helpless thing made by men that could neither hear, see, nor speak; and that such a stupid thing could no ways hurt or help them. To this he answered very unwillingly and with much hesitation. However, he at last delivered himself in these broken and imperfect sentences: "It is the priests—they make the people believe and—" Here he paused a little and then repeated to me that "it was the priests—" and then gave me hopes that he would have said something more, but a qualm crossed his conscience and hindered him from making any further concession.

The priests and conjurers have a great sway in every nation. Their words are looked upon as oracles and consequently are of great weight among the common people. They perform their adorations and conjurations in the general language before spoken of, as the Catholics of all nations do their mass in the Latin. They teach that the souls of men survive their bodies, and that those who have done well here enjoy most transporting pleasures in their Elysium hereafter; that this Elysium is stored with the highest perfection of all their earthly pleasures—namely, with plenty of all sorts of game for hunting, fishing, and fowling; that it is blest with the most charming women which enjoy an eternal bloom and have a universal desire to please; that it is delivered from excesses of cold or heat and flourishes with an everlasting spring. But that on the contrary those who are wicked and live scandalously here are condemned to a filthy, stinking lake after death that continually burns with flames that never extinguish, where they are persecuted and tormented day and night with furies in the shape of old women.

They use many divinations and enchantments and frequently offer burnt sacrifice to the evil spirit. The people annually present their first fruits of every season and kind; namely, of birds, beasts, fish, fruits, plants, roots, and of all other things which they esteem either of profit or pleasure to themselves. They repeat their offerings as frequently as they have great successes in their wars or their fishing, fowling, or hunting.

Some few years ago there happened a very dry time towards the heads of the rivers and especially on the upper parts of James River where Colonel Byrd had several quarters of Negroes. This gentleman has for a long time been extremely respected and feared by all the Indians round about, who, without knowing the name of any governor, have ever been kept in order by him. During this drought an Indian well known to one of the colonel's overseers came to him and asked if his tobacco was not like to be spoiled? The overseer answered yes, if they had not rain very suddenly. The Indian, who pretended great kindness for his master, told the overseer if he would promise to give him two bottles of rum he would bring him rain enough. The overseer did not believe anything of the matter, not seeing at that time the least appearance of rain nor so much as a cloud in the sky. However, he promised to give him the rum when his master came thither if he would be as good as his word. Upon this the Indian went immediately a-pow-wowing, as they call it, and in about half an hour there came up a black cloud into the sky that showered down rain enough upon this gentleman's corn and tobacco, but none at all upon any of the neighbors except a few drops of the skirt of the shower. The Indian for that time went away without returning to the overseer again till he heard of his master's arrival at the falls, and then he came to him and demanded the two bottles of rum. The colonel at first seemed to know nothing of the matter and asked the Indian for what reason he made that demand (altho' his overseer had been so overjoyed at what had happened that he could not rest till he had taken a horse and rid near forty miles to tell his master the story). The Indian answered with some concern that he hoped the overseer had let him know the service he had done him by bringing a shower of rain to save his crop. At this the colonel, not being apt to believe such stories, smiled and told him he was a cheat and had seen the cloud a-coming, otherwise he could neither have brought rain nor so much as foretold it. The Indian, at this seeming much troubled, replied: "Why, then, had not such a one and such a one (naming the next neighbors) rain as well as your overseer, for they lost their crops; but I loved you and therefore saved yours?" The colonel made sport with him a little while, but in the end ordered him the two bottles of rum, letting him understand, however, that it was a free gift and not the consequence of any bargain with his overseer.

The solemnity of huskanawing is commonly practiced once every fourteen or sixteen years or oftener as their young men happen to grow up. It is an institution or discipline which all young men must pass before they can be admitted to be of the number of the great men or cockarouses of the nation. The whole ceremony is performed after the following manner.

The choicest and briskest young men of the town and such only as have acquired some treasure by their travels and hunting are chosen out by the rulers to be huskanawed, and whoever refuses to undergo this process dare not remain among them. The principal part of the business is to carry them into the woods and there keep them under confinement and destitute of all society for several months, giving them no other sustenance but the infusion or decoction of some poisonous intoxicating roots; by virtue of which physic and by the severity of the discipline which they undergo they become stark staring mad, in which raving condition they are kept eighteen or twenty days. During these extremities they are shut up night and day in a strong enclosure made on purpose; one of which I saw, belonging to the Paumunkey Indians, in the year 1694. It was in shape like a sugar loaf and every way open like a lattice for the air to pass through. In this cage thirteen young men had been huskanawed and had not been a month set at liberty when I saw it. Upon this occasion it is pretended that these poor creatures drink so much of that water of Lethe that they perfectly lose the remembrance of all former things, even of their parents, their treasure, and their language. When the doctors find that they have drank sufficiently of the wysoccan (so they call this made potion) they gradually restore them to their senses again by lessening the intoxication of their diet. But before they are perfectly well they bring them back into their towns while they are still wild and crazy through the violence of the medicine. After this they are very fearful of discovering anything of their former remembrance, for if such a thing should happen to any of them, they must immediately be huskanawed again, and the second time the usage is so severe that seldom anyone escapes with life. Thus they must pretend to have forgot the very use of their tongues so as not to be able to speak nor understand anything that is spoken till they learn it again. Now whether this be real or counterfeit I don't know, but certain it is that they will not for some time take notice of anybody nor anything with which they were before acquainted, being still under the guard of their keepers, who constantly wait upon them everywhere till they have learnt all things perfectly over again. Thus they unlive their former lives and commence men by forgetting that they ever have been boys.

I can account no other way for the great pains and secrecy of the keepers during the whole process of this discipline but by assuring you that it is the most meritorious thing in the world to discharge that trust well in order to their preferment to the greatest posts in the nation, which they claim as their undoubted right in the next promotion. On the other hand, they are sure of a speedy passport into the other world if they should by their levity or neglect show themselves in the least unfaithful.

Those which I ever observed to have been huskanawed were lively, handsome, well timbered young men from fifteen to twenty years of age or upward, and such as were generally reputed rich.

I confess I judged it at first sight to be only an invention of the seniors to engross the young men's riches to themselves, for after suffering this operation they never pretended to call to mind anything of their former property. But their goods were either shared among the old men or brought to some public use, and so those younkers [young gentlemen] were obliged to begin the world again.

But the Indians detest this opinion and pretend that this violent method of taking away the memory is to release the youth from all their childish impressions and from that strong partiality to persons and things which is contracted before reason comes to take place. They hope by this proceeding to root out all the prepossessions and unreasonable prejudices which are fixed in the minds of children, so that when the young men come to themselves again their reason may act freely without being bypassed by the cheats of custom and education. Thus also they become discharged from the remembrance of any ties by blood and are established in a state of equality and perfect freedom to order their actions and dispose of their persons as they think fit without any other control than that of the law of nature. By this means also they become qualified when they have any public office equally and impartially to administer justice without having respect either to friend or relation.

The Indians offer sacrifice almost upon every new occasion— as when they travel or begin a long journey, they burn tobacco instead of incense to the sun to bribe him to send them fair weather and a prosperous voyage. When they cross any great water or violent fresh or torrent they throw tobacco, puccoon, peak, or some other valuable thing that they happen to have about them to entreat the spirit presiding there to grant them a safe passage. It is called a fresh when after very great rains or (as we suppose) after a great thaw of the snow and ice lying upon the mountains to the northwest the water descends in such abundance into the rivers that they overflow the banks which bound their streams at other times.

They make their account by units—tens, hundreds, etc.—as we do, but they reckon the years by the winters, or cohonks as they call them, which is a name taken from the note of the wild geese, intimating so many times of the wild geese coming to them, which is every winter. They distinguish the several parts of the year by five seasons, viz., the budding or blossoming of the spring; the earing of the corn or roasting ear time; the summer or highest sun; the corn gathering or fall of the leaf; and the winter or cohonks. They count the months likewise by the moons, tho' not with any relation to so many in a year as we do, but they make them return again by the same name, as the Moon of Stags, the Corn Moon, the first and second moon of cohonks, etc. They have no distinction of the hours of the day, but divide it only into three parts— the rise, power, and lowering of the sun. And they keep their account by knots on a string or notches on a stick, not unlike the Peruvian quippoes.

In this state of nature one would think they should be as pure from superstition and overdoing matters in religion as they are in other things; but I find it is quite the contrary, for this simplicity gives the cunning priest a greater advantage over them, according to the Romish maxim, "Ignorance is the mother of devotion." For no bigoted pilgrim appears more zealous or strains his devotion more at the shrine than these believing Indians do in their idolatrous adorations. Neither do the most refined Catholics undergo their penance with so much submission as these poor pagans do the severities which their priests inflict upon them.

The conjurer is a partner with the priest not only in the cheat but in the advantages of it, and sometimes they officiate for one another. When this artist is in the act of conjuration, or of powwowing as they term it, he always appears with an air of haste or else in some convulsive posture that seems to strain all the faculties, like the sybils when they pretend to be under the power of inspiration. At these times he has a black bird with expanded wings fastened to his ear, differing in nothing but color from Mahomet's pigeon. He has no clothing but a small skin before and a pocket at his girdle.

The Indians never go about any considerable enterprise without first consulting their priests and conjurers, for the most ingenious amongst them are brought up to those functions, and by that means become better instructed in their histories than the rest of the people. They likewise engross to themselves all the knowledge of nature which is handed to them by tradition from their forefathers, by which means they are able to make a truer judgment of things and consequently are more capable of advising those that consult them upon all occasions. These reverend gentlemen are not so entirely given up to their religious austerities but they sometimes take their pleasure (as well as the laity) in fishing, fowling, and hunting.

The Indians have posts fixed round their quioccasan which have men's faces carved upon them and are painted. They are likewise set up round some of their other celebrated places and make a circle for them to dance about on certain solemn occasions. They very often set up pyramidical stones and pillars which they color with puccoon and other sorts of paint, and which they adorn with peak, roanoke, etc. To these they pay all outward signs of worship and devotion, not as to God, but as they are hieroglyphics of the permanency and immutability of the deity—because these both for figure and substance are of all sublunary bodies the least subject to decay or change. They also for the same reason keep baskets of stones in their cabins. Upon this account, too, they offer sacrifice to running streams, which by the perpetuity of their motion typify the eternity of God.

The Indians are religious in preserving the corpses of their kings and rulers after death, which they order in the following manner: First, they neatly flay off the skin as entire as they can, slitting it only in the back; then they pick all the flesh off from the bones as clean as possible, leaving the sinews fastened to the bones that they may preserve the joints together; then they dry the bones a little in the sun and put them into the skin again, which in the meantime has been kept from drying or shrinking. When the bones are placed right in the skin, they nicely fill up the vacuities with a very fine white sand. After this they sew up the skin again and the body looks as if the flesh had not been removed. They take care to keep the skin from shrinking by the help of a little oil or grease, which saves it also from corruption. The skin being thus prepared, they lay it in an apartment for that purpose upon a large shelf raised above the floor. This shelf is spread with mats for the corpse to rest easy on and screened with the same to keep it from the dust. The flesh they lay upon hurdles in the sun to dry, and when it is thoroughly dried it is sewed up in a basket and set at the feet of the corpse to which it belongs. In this place also they set up a quioccos, or idol, which they believe will be a guard to the corpse. Here night and day one or other of the priests must give his attendance to take care of the dead bodies, so great an honor and veneration have these ignorant and unpolished people for their princes, even after they are dead.

9

Of the Diseases and Cures of the Indians

The Indians are not subject to many diseases, and such as they have generally come from excessive heats and sudden colds, which they as suddenly get away by sweating. But if the humor happen to fix and make a pain in any particular joint or limb, their general cure then is by burning, if it be in any part that will bear it. Their method of doing this is by little sticks of lightwood, the coal of which will burn like a hot iron. The sharp point of this they run into the flesh, and having made a sore keep it running till the humor be drawn off. Or else they take punk, which is a sort of a soft touchwood cut out of the knots of oak or hickory trees, but the hickory affords the best. This they shape like a cone (as the Japanese do their moxa for the gout) and apply the basis of it to the place affected. Then they set fire to it, letting it burn out upon the part which makes a running sore effectually.

They use sucking frequently, and scarifying which, like the Mexicans, they perform with a rattlesnake's tooth. They seldom cut deeper than the epidermis, by which means they give passage to those sharp waterish humors that lie between the two skins and cause inflammations. Sometimes they make use of reeds for cauterizing, which they heat over the fire till they are ready to flame and then apply them upon a piece of thin wet leather to the place aggrieved, which makes the heat more piercing.

Their priests are always physicians, and by the method of their education in the priesthood are made very knowing in the hidden quality of plants and other natural things which they count a part of their religion to conceal from everybody but from those that are to succeed them in their holy function. They tell us their God will be angry with them if they should discover that part of their knowledge, so they suffer only the rattlesnake root to be known and such other antidotes as must be immediately applied, because their doctors can't be always at hand to remedy those sudden misfortunes which generally happen in their hunting or traveling.

The physic of the Indians consists for the most part in the roots and barks of trees, they very rarely using the leaves either of herbs or trees. What they give inwardly they infuse in water, and what they apply outwardly they stamp or bruise, adding water to it if it has not moisture enough of itself; with the thin of this they bathe the part affected, then lay on the thick after the manner of a poultice and commonly dress round, leaving the fore place bare.

They take great delight in sweating and therefore in every town they have a sweating house, and a doctor is paid by the public to attend it. They commonly use this to refresh themselves after they have been fatigued with hunting, travel, or the like, or else when they are troubled with agues, aches, or pains in their limbs. Their method is thus: The doctor takes three or four large stones which after having heated red hot, he places 'em in the middle of the stove, laying on them some of the inner bark of oak beaten in a mortar to keep them from burning. This being done, they creep in six or eight at a time, or as many as the place will hold, and then close up the mouth of the stove, which is usually made like an oven, in some bank near the waterside. In the meanwhile, the doctor to raise a steam after they have been stewing a little while pours cold water on the stones and now and then sprinkles the men to keep them from fainting. After they have sweat as long as they can well endure it, they sally out and (tho' it be in the depth of winter) forthwith plunge themselves over head and ears in cold water, which instantly closes up the pores and preserves them from taking cold. The heat being thus suddenly driven from the extreme parts to the heart, makes them a little feeble for the present, but their spirits rally again, and they instantly recover their strength and find their joints as supple and vigorous as if they never had traveled or been indisposed.

10

Of the Sports and Pastimes of the Indians

Their sports and pastimes are singing, dancing, instrumental music, and some boisterous plays which are performed by running, catching, and leaping upon one another. They have also one great diversion, to the practicing of which are requisite whole handfuls of sticks or hard straws which they know how to count as fast as they can cast their eyes upon them and can handle with a surprising dexterity.

Their singing is not the most charming that I have heard. It consists much in exalting the voice and is full of slow melancholy accents. However, I must allow even this music to contain some wild notes that are agreeable.

Their dancing is performed either by few or a great company, but without much regard either to time or figure. The first of these is by one or two persons or at most by three. In the meanwhile, the company sit about them in a ring upon the ground singing outrageously and shaking their rattles. The dancers sometimes sing and sometimes look menacing and terrible, beating their feet furiously against the ground and showing ten thousand grimaces and distortions. The other is performed by a great number of people, the dancers themselves forming a ring and moving round a circle of carved posts that are set up for that purpose, or else round a fire made in a convenient part of the town; and then each has his rattle in his hand or what other thing he fancies most, as his bow and arrows or his tomahawk. They also dress themselves up with branches of trees or some other strange accoutrements. Thus they proceed, dancing and singing with all the antic postures they can invent; and he's the bravest fellow that has the most prodigious gestures.

They have a fire made constantly every night at a convenient place in the town, whither all that have a mind to be merry at the public dance or music resort in the evening.

Their musical instruments are chiefly drums and rattles. Their drums are made of a skin stretched over an earthen pot half full of water. Their rattles are the shell of a small gourd or macock of the creeping kind and not of those called calabashes which grow upon trees; of which the Brazilians make their maraca or tamaraka, a sort of rattle also, as L'Ecluse seems to intimate.

11

Of the Laws and Authority
of the Indians
Among One Another

The Indians having no sort of letters among them, as has been before observed, they can have no written laws. Nor did the constitution in which we found them seem to need many, nature and their own convenience having taught them to obey one chief who is arbiter of all things among them. They claim no property in lands, but they are in common to a whole nation. Everyone hunts and fishes and gathers fruits in all places. Their labor in tending corn, pompions, melons, etc., is not so great that they need quarrel for room where the land is so fertile and where so much lies uncultivated.

They bred no sort of cattle nor had anything that could be called riches. They valued skins and furs for use and peak and roanoke for ornament.

They are very severe in punishing ill breeding, of which every werowance is undisputed judge, who never fails to lay a rigorous penalty upon it. An example whereof I had from a gentleman that was an eye witness, which was this:

In the time of Bacon's Rebellion, one of these werowances, attended by several others of his nation, was treating with the English in New Kent County about a peace. And during the time of his speech one of his attendants presumed to interrupt him, which he resented as the most unpardonable affront that could be offered him; and therefore he instantly took his tomahawk from his girdle and split the fellow's head for his presumption. The poor fellow dying immediately upon the spot, he commanded some of his men to carry him out and went on again with his speech where he left off as unconcerned as if nothing had happened.

The Indians never forget nor forgive an injury till satisfaction be given, be it national or personal. But it becomes the business of their whole lives, and even after that the revenge is entailed upon their posterity till full reparation be made.

The titles of honor that I have observed among them peculiar to themselves are only cockarouse and werowance besides that of the king and queen. But of late they have borrowed some titles from us which they bestow among themselves. A cockarouse is one that has the honor to be of the king or queen's council with relation to the affairs of the government and has a great share in the administration. A werowance is a military officer who, of course, takes upon him the command of all parties either of hunting, traveling, warring, or the like, and the word signifies a war captain.

The priests and conjurers are also of great authority; the people having recourse to them for counsel and direction upon all occasions, by which means and by help of the first fruits and frequent offerings they riot in the fat of the land and grow rich upon the spoils of their ignorant countrymen.

They have also people of a rank inferior to the commons, a sort of servants among them. These are called black boys and are attendant upon the gentry to do their servile offices, which in their seat of nature are not many. For they live barely up to the present relief of their necessities and make all things easy and comfortable to themselves by the indulgence of a kind climate without toiling and perplexing their mind for riches, which other people often trouble themselves to provide for uncertain and ungrateful heirs. In short, they seem as possessing nothing and yet enjoying all things.

12

Of the Treasure or Riches of the Indians

The Indians had nothing which they reckoned riches before the English went among them except peak, roanoke, and such like trifles made out of the conch shell. These passed with them instead of gold and silver and served them both for money and ornament. It was the English alone that taught them first to put a value on their skins and furs and to make a trade of them.

Peak is of two sorts, or rather of two colors, for both are made of one shell tho' of different parts. One is a dark purple cylinder and the other a white. They are both made in size and figure alike and commonly much resembling the English bugles [glass beads] but not so transparent nor so brittle. They are wrought as smooth as glass, being one third of an inch long and about a quarter diameter, strung by a hole drilled thro' the center. The dark color is the dearest and distinguished by the name of wampum peak. The Englishmen that are called Indian traders value the wampum peak at eighteen pence per yard and the white peak at nine pence. The Indians also make pipes of this two or three inches long and thicker than ordinary, which are much more valuable.

They have also another sort which is as current among them but of far less value. And this is made of the cockleshell broke into small bits with rough edges, drilled through in the same manner as beads, and this they call roanoke, and use it as the peak.

These sorts of money have their rates set upon them as unalterable and current as the values of our money are.

The Indians have likewise some pearl amongst them and formerly had many more, but where they got them is uncertain, except they found 'em in the oyster banks which are frequent in this country.

13

Of the Handicrafts
of the Indians

Before I finish my account of the Indians, it will not be amiss to inform you that when the English went first among them they had no sort of iron or steel instruments; but their knives were either sharpened reeds or shells, and their axes sharp stones bound to the end of a stick and glued in with turpentine. By the help of these they made their bows of the locust tree, an excessive hard wood when it is dry but much more easily cut when it is green, of which they always took the advantage. They made their arrows of reeds or small wands which need no other cutting but in the length, being otherwise ready for notching, feathering, and heading. They fledged their arrows with turkey feathers which they fastened with glue made of the velvet horns of a deer, but it has not that quality it's said to have of holding against all weathers. They armed the heads with a white transparent stone like that of Mexico mentioned by Peter Martyr, of which they have many rocks; they also headed them with spurs of the wild turkey cock.

They rubbed fire out of particular sorts of wood (as the ancients did out of the ivy and bays) by turning the end of a hard piece upon the side of a piece that is soft and dry, like a spindle on its ink, by which it heats and at length burns. To this they put sometimes also rotten wood and dry leaves to hasten the work.

Under the disadvantage of such tools they made a shift to fell vast great trees and clear the land of wood in places where they had occasion.

They bring down a great tree by making a small fire round the root and keeping the flame from running upward until they burn away so much of the basis that the least puff of wind throws it down. When it is prostrate they burn it off to what length they would have it, and with their stone tomahawks break off all the bark, which when the sap runs will easily strip, and at other times also if it be well warmed with fire. When it is brought to a due length, they raise it upon a bed to a convenient height for their working and then begin by gentle fires to hollow it and with scrapers rake the trunk and turn away the fire from one place to another till they have deepened the belly of it to their desire. Thus also they shape the ends till they have made it a fit vessel for crossing the water, and this they call a canoe, one of which I have seen thirty foot long.

When they wanted any land to be cleared of the woods, they chopped a notch round the trees quite through the bark with their stone hatchets or tomahawks, and that deadened the trees so that they sprouted no more but in a few years fell down. However, the ground was plantable and would produce immediately upon the withering of the trees. But now for all these uses they employ axes and little hatchets, which they buy of the English. The occasions aforementioned and the building of their cabins are still the greatest use they have for these utensils because they trouble not themselves with any other sort of handicraft to which such tools are necessary. Their household utensils are baskets made of silk grass, gourds which grow to the shapes they desire them, and earthen pots to boil victuals in which they make of clay.

The Indians of Virginia are almost wasted—all which together can't raise five hundred fighting men. They live poorly and much in fear of the neighboring Indians. Each town, by the articles of peace in 1677, pays three Indian arrows for their land and twenty beaver skins for protection every year.

Thus I have given a succinct account of the Indians—happy, I think in their simple state of nature and in their enjoyment of plenty without the curse of labor. They have on several accounts reason to lament the arrival of the Europeans, by whose means they seem to have lost their felicity as well as their innocence. The English have taken away great part of their country and consequently made everything less plenty amongst them. They have introduced drunkenness and luxury amongst them, which have multiplied their wants and put them upon desiring a thousand things they never dreamt of before. I shall in the next place proceed to treat of Virginia as it is now improved (I should rather say altered) by the English, and of its present constitution and settlement.

BOOK FOUR

Of the Present State of Virginia.

As This Book Must Consist of Two Parts, First, the Polity of the Government, Secondly, the Husbandry and Improvements of the Country, so I Shall Handle Them Separately.

PART I

OF THE CIVIL POLITY AND GOVERNMENT OF VIRGINIA

1

Of the Constitution of Government in Virginia

Before the year 1680 the Council sat in the same house with the burgesses of Assembly, much resembling the model of the Scots Parliament. And then the Lord Culpeper, taking advantage of some disputes among them, procured the Council to sit apart from the Assembly, and so they became two distinct houses in imitation of the two houses of Parliament in England—the Lords and Commons. And so is the constitution at this day.

The governor is appointed by the Crown; his commission is under the Privy Seal and runs during pleasure.

He represents the queen's person there in all things and is subject to her instructions.

In assenting to or dissenting from the laws agreed upon by the Council and Assembly.

In giving his test to all laws so assented to.

In calling, proroguing, and dissolving the Assembly.

In calling and presiding in all Councils of State.

In appointing commissioners and officers for the administration of justice.

In granting commissions to all officers of the militia under the degree of a lieutenant general, which title he bears himself.

In ordering and disposing the militia for the defense of the country, according to law.

In testing proclamations.

In disposing of the queen's land according to the charter and the laws of that country; for which end, and for other public occasions, the seal of the colony is committed to his keeping.

All issues of the public revenue must bear his test.

And by virtue of a commission from the Admiralty he takes upon himself the office of vice admiral.

The governor's salary till within these thirty years last past was no more than a thousand pounds a year; besides which he had about five hundred more in perquisites. Indeed, the General Assembly by a public act made an addition of two hundred pounds a year to Sir William Berkeley in particular, out of the great respect and esteem they bore to that gentleman who had been a long time a good and just governor and who had laid out the greatest part of his revenue in experiments for the advantage and improvement of the country, and who had besides suffered extremely in the time of the usurpation. But this addition was to determine [terminate] with his government.

Sir William Berkeley, after the short interval of Jefferys' and Chicheley's being deputy governors, was succeeded by the Lord Culpeper, who under the pretense of his being a peer of England obtained of King Charles II a salary of £2,000 besides £150 a year for house rent because there was no house appointed by the country for the governor's reception.

This noble lord made his advantage of the confusions in which he found the country that had not recovered the calamities of Bacon's Rebellion. He observed that [an] abundance of people had been concerned in those troubles, and consequently he concluded they would not scruple to grant him anything to protect themselves from prosecution. By this means he not only obtained the concurrence of the Assembly to his money grants, but likewise prevailed with them to make the imposition of two shillings per hogshead and the fort duties perpetual and to make them subject to his Majesty's direction, to be disposed of for the use of the government. This increased salary has been continued ever since, to all the succeeding governors, and the perquisites are now also increased.

The gentlemen of the Council are appointed by letter or instruction from her Majesty, which says no more but that they be sworn of the Council.

The number of the councilors when complete is twelve. And if at any time by death or removal there happen to be fewer than nine residing in the country, then the governor has power to appoint and swear into the Council such of the gentlemen of the country as he shall think fit to make up that number without expecting any direction from England.

The business of the Council is to advise and assist the governor in all important matters of government and to be a restraint upon him if he should attempt to exceed the bounds of his commission. They are enabled to do this by having each of them an equal vote with the governor in most things of consequence, viz.,

In calling Assemblies.

In disposing of the public revenue and inspecting the accounts thereof.

In placing and displacing naval officers and collectors of all public duties.

In all votes and orders of Council.

In the nomination of all commissioned officers, either of honorary or profitable places.

In publishing proclamations.

In making grants and passing all the patents for land.

In the General Assembly, the Council make the upper house and claim an entire negative voice to all laws, as the House of Lords in England.

The salary of the Council is in all about £350 per annum to be proportioned among them according to their attendance on general courts and Assemblies.

The burgesses of Assembly are elected and returned from all parts of the country, viz., from each county two and from James City one; which make up in all fifty-one burgesses, besides one burgess to be sent by the College, as the charter directs. They are convened by writs issued from the secretary's office under the seal of the colony and the test of the governor. These are directed to the sheriff of each county respectively, and ought to bear date at least forty days before the return. The freeholders are the only electors, and wherever they have a freehold (if they be not women or under age) they have a vote in the election. The method of summoning the freeholders is by publication of the writ together with the day appointed by the sheriff for election at every church and chapel in the county, two several Sundays successively. The election is concluded by plurality of voices, and if either party be dissatisfied or thinks he has not fair treatment he may demand a copy of the poll and upon application to the House of Burgesses shall have his complaint inquired into. But to prevent undue elections, many acts have been there made agreeable to some lately enacted in England.

The first business of a convention is to make choice of a speaker and to present him in full house to the governor. Upon this occasion the speaker in the name of the house petitions the governor to confirm the usual liberties and privileges of assembly, namely, access to his person whenever they shall have occasion, a freedom of speech and debate in the house without being further accountable, and a protection of their persons and their servants from arrest, etc. And these being granted by the governor, they proceed to do business, choosing committees and in other things imitating as near as they can the method of the honorable House of Commons in England.

The laws having duly passed the House of Burgesses, the Council, and the governor's assent, they are transmitted to the queen by the next shipping for her approbation, her Majesty having another negative voice on this condition: that they immediately become laws and be in force upon the governor's first passing them and so remain if her Majesty don't actually repeal them, although she be not pleased to declare her royal assent.

There are no appointed times for their convention, but the custom hitherto has been once in a year or once in two years. And, indeed, seldom two entire years pass without an Assembly, they wisely keeping the power that is left them in their own hands by the short continuation of the imposition acts. They are called together whenever the exigencies of the country make it necessary, or her Majesty is pleased to order anything to be proposed to them.

2

Of the Sub-Divisions of Virginia

The country is divided into twenty-five counties, and the counties as they are in bigness into fewer or more parishes.

The method of bounding the counties is at this time with respect to the convenience of having each county limited to one single river for its trade and shipping, so that anyone whose concerns are altogether in one county may not be obliged to seek his freight and shipping in more than one river; whereas at first they were bounded with respect to the circuit and the propinquity of the extremes to one common center, by which means one county reached then quite across a neck of land from river to river. But this way of bounding the counties being found more inconvenient than the other, it was changed by law into what it is now.

Besides this division into counties and parishes, there are two other sub-divisions which are subject to the rules and alterations made by the county courts: namely, into precincts or boroughs for the limits of constables, and into precincts or walks for the surveyors of highways.

3

Of the Public Offices of Government

Besides the governor and Council aforementioned, there are two other general officers in that colony bearing her Majesty's immediate commission, viz., the auditor of the revenue and the secretary of state.

The auditor's business is to audit the accounts of the public money of the government and duly to transmit the state of them to England, such as the quitrents, the money arising by the two shillings per hogshead, fort duties, the fines and forfeitures, and the profits of escheats. His salary is 7½ per cent of all the public money.

The secretary's business is to keep the public records of the country and to take care that they be regularly and fairly made up; namely, all judgments of the general court as likewise all deeds and other writings there proved; and further, to issue all writs, both ministerial and judicial relating thereto, to make out and record all patents for land, to file the rights by which they issued, and to take the return of all inquests of escheat.

In his office is kept a register of all commissions of administration and probates of wills granted throughout the colony; as also of all births, burials, marriages, and persons that go out of the country; of all houses of public entertainment, and of all public officers in the country; and of many other things proper to be kept in so general an office.

From this office are likewise issued all writs for choosing burgesses, and in it are filed authentic copies of all proclamations.

This office was reduced into very good order after the burning of the State House at Jamestown, but for want of conveniences and due care it is growing apace into as great confusion as ever.

The secretary's income arises from fees for all business done in his office, which come (*communibus annis*) to about seventy thousand pounds of tobacco per annum; out of which he pays 12,500 and cask to the clerks. His other perquisites proceed out of the acknowledgements paid him annually by the county clerks and are besides about forty thousand pounds a year of tobacco and cask.

There are two other general officers in the country who do not receive their commission and authority immediately from the crown, and those are: 1. The ecclesiastical commissary, authorized by the Right Reverend Father in God, the Lord Bishop of London, ordinary of all the plantations; 2. the country's treasurer, authorized by the General Assembly.

The commissary's business is to make visitations of churches and have the inspection of the clergy. He is allowed one hundred pounds per annum out of the quitrents.

The treasurer's business is to receive the money from the several collectors and to make up the accounts of the duties raised by some late acts of Assembly for extraordinary occasions. His salary is six per cent of all money passing through his hands.

These are all the general officers belonging to that government, except of the court of admiralty which has no standing officer.

The other public commission officers in the government (except those of the militia, for whom a chapter is reserved) are escheators, naval officers, collectors, clerks of courts, sheriffs of counties, surveyors of land, and coroners.

The escheators have their precincts or bounds according to the several necks of land; for their profits they demand five pounds sterling for each office found, being paid only as business happens.

The naval officers have their bounds according to the districts on the rivers and so have the collectors. The profits of the first arise from large fees upon the entering and clearing of all ships and vessels. The collectors have each a salary out of the treasury in England of £40, £60, or £100, according to their several districts, they being appointed by the honorable the Commissioners of Customs in England pursuant to a statute made in the twenty-fifth year of King Charles II; and have moreover salaries of twenty per cent on all the duties they collect by virtue of the same statute, and also large fees for every entry and clearing.

The naval officers' other profits are ten per cent for all monies by them received both on the two shillings per hogshead, fort duties, skins and furs, and also on the new imposts on servants and liquors.

The clerks of courts, sheriffs, and surveyors are limited according to the several counties. The clerks of courts receive their commissions from the secretary of state; the sheriffs, theirs from the governor; and the surveyors of land, theirs from the governors of the College in whom the office of surveyor general is vested by their charter.

The clerks' profits proceed from stated fees upon all lawsuits and business in their respective courts except the clerk of the general court who is paid a salary by the secretary who takes the fees of that court to himself. The large and populous counties by these fees allow a plentiful maintenance to their clerks. The clerks at present exact what fees they will, having none allowed them by law because of the expiration of the acts relating thereto.

The sheriff's profit is likewise by fees on all business done in the county courts to which he is the ministerial officer, but the best of his income is by a salary of ten per cent on all his collections. He has likewise several other advantages which make his place very profitable.

The profits of the surveyors of land are according to the trouble they take; but because men of honor and understanding should be encouraged to undertake this office, on whose probity and skill the title and quiet of estates depend, it were to be wished that these officers were allowed larger fees.

The coroner is a commission officer also, but his profits are not worth naming, though he has large fees allowed him when he does any business. There are two or more of them appointed in each parish as occasion requires, but in the vacancy or absence of any upon exigency, the next justice of peace does the business and receives the fee which is 133 pounds of tobacco for an inquest and nothing for any other business.

There are other ministerial officers that have no commission which are: surveyors of the highways, constables, and headboroughs. These are appointed, relieved, and altered annually by the county courts as they see occasion, and such bounds are given them as those courts think most convenient. Their business is all done without profit.

4

Of the Standing Revenues or Public Funds in Virginia

There are five sorts of standing public revenues in that country; viz., first, a rent reserved by her Majesty upon all the lands granted by patent; second, a revenue granted to her Majesty by act of Assembly for the support and maintenance of the government; third, a revenue raised by the Assembly and kept in their own disposal for extraordinary occasions; fourth, a revenue raised by the Assembly and granted to the College; and fifth, a revenue raised by act of Parliament in England upon the trade there.

First, the rent reserved upon their lands is called her Majesty's revenue of quitrents, and is two shillings for every hundred acres of land patented by any person in that country. This is paid into the treasury there by all, except the inhabitants of the Northern Neck, who pay nothing to the queen; but the whole quitrent of that Neck is paid to certain proprietors of the Lord Culpeper's family, who have assumed the possession thereof to themselves, upon the pretensions before rehearsed in the first part of this book.

This revenue has been upwards of twelve hundred pounds a year since tobacco has held a good price. It is lodged in the auditor's hands to be disposed of by her Majesty to the use and benefit of the country. This money is left in bank there to be made use of upon any sudden and dangerous emergency. And for want of such a bank Sir William Berkeley was not able to make any stand against Bacon, whom otherwise he might easily have subdued and consequently have prevented above £100,000 expense to the Crown of England to pacify those troubles.

Second, the revenue granted to her Majesty by act of Assembly for the support and maintenance of the government arises first out of a duty of two shillings per hogshead which is paid for every hogshead of tobacco exported out of that colony; secondly, by a rate of fifteen pence per ton for every ship upon each return of her voyage, whether she be empty or full; thirdly, by a duty of sixpence per poll for every passenger, bond or free, going into that country; fourthly, by the fines and forfeitures imposed by several acts of Assembly; fifthly, by waifs and strays happening to be taken up within that government; and sixthly, by escheats of land and personal estate for want of a lawful heir. All which are paid into the hands of the auditor and disposed of by the governor and Council (with liberty for the Assembly to inspect the accounts when they meet) for defraying the public charges of the government.

This revenue, *communibus annis*, amounts to more than £3,000 a year.

Third, the revenue arising by act of Assembly and reserved to their own disposal is of two sorts; viz., a duty upon liquors imported from the neighboring plantations and a duty upon all slaves and servants imported except English.

The duty on liquors is 4*d.* per gallon on all wines, rum, and brandy; and 1*d.* per gallon on beer, cider, and other liquors, discounting twenty per cent upon the invoice.

The duty on servants and slaves is 15 shillings for each servant not being a native of England or Wales, and 20 shillings for each slave or Negro.

The former of these duties amounts *communibus annis* to £600

a year, and the latter to more or less as the Negro ships happen
to arrive.

The charge of building and adorning the capitol was defrayed
by the last of these duties and so was the erecting of the public
prison. By both these several great claimers from the Assembly
are paid, which would ease the levy by the poll if the duty were
raised any other way than upon the servants. But the latter of
these being a duty of 15 or 20 shillings per head, makes it advance
to forty or fifty in the sale, as hath been experienced, and so there's
five or six years' levy paid before the servant can be purchased.

These funds are gathered into the hands of the treasurer of the
country and are disposed of only by order of Assembly.

Fourthly, the revenue raised by the Assembly and granted to
the College is a duty on all skins and furs exported. This fund
raises about a hundred pounds a year and is paid by the collectors
to the College treasurer.

Fifthly and lastly, the fund raised by act of Parliament in England upon the trade there is a duty of one penny per pound upon
all tobacco exported to the plantations and not carried directly to
England. This duty was laid by *Stat. 25. Car. 2 cap. 7* and granted
to the king and his successors, and by their gracious Majesties
King William and Queen Mary it was given to the College. This
duty does not raise both in Virginia and Maryland above two
hundred pounds a year and is accounted for to the College
treasurer.

5

Of the Levies for Payment
of the Public, County,
and Parish Debts

They have but two ways of raising money publicly in that
country; viz., by duties upon trade, and a poll tax which they call
levies. Of the duties upon trade I have spoken sufficiently in the
preceding chapter. I come therefore now to speak of the levies
which are a certain rate or proportion of tobacco charged upon
the head of every tithable person in the country upon all alike
without distinction.

They call Negroes above sixteen years of age tithable, be they male or female, and all white men of the same age. But children and white women are exempted from all manner of duties.

That a true account of all these tithable persons may be had, they are annually listed in crop time by the justices of each county respectively; and the masters of families are obliged under great penalties then to deliver to those justices a true list of all the tithable persons in their families.

Their levies are of three sorts, viz., public, county, and parish levies.

Public levies are such as are proportioned and laid equally by the General Assembly upon every tithable person throughout the whole colony. These serve to defray several expenses appointed by law to be so defrayed, such as the executing of a criminal slave who must be made good to his owner, the taking up of runaways, and the paying of the militia when they happen to be employed upon service. Out of these they likewise pay the several officers of the Assembly and some other public officers. They further defray the charge of the writs for the meeting of the House of Burgesses and such like.

The authority for levying this rate is given by a short act of Assembly constantly prepared for that purpose.

The county levies are such as are peculiar to each county and laid by the justices upon all tithable persons for defraying the charge of their counties, such as the building and repairing their courthouses, prisons, pillories, stocks, etc., and the payment of all services rendered to the county in general.

The parish levies are laid by the vestry for the payment of all charges incident to the several parishes, such as the building, furnishing, and adorning their churches and chapels, buying glebes and building upon them, paying their ministers, readers, clerks, and sextons.

6

Of the Courts of Law in Virginia

The general court from the beginning took cognizance of all causes whatsoever, both ecclesiastical and civil, determining everything by the standard of equity and good conscience. They used to come to the merits of the cause as soon as they could without injustice, never admitting such impertinences of form and nicety as were not absolutely necessary, and when the substance of the case was sufficiently debated they used directly to bring the suit to a decision. By this method all fair actions were prosecuted with little attendance, all just debts were recovered with the least expense of money and time, and all the tricking and foppery of the law happily avoided.

The Lord Culpeper, who was a man of admirable sense and well skilled in the laws of England, admired the constitution of their courts and kept them close to this plain method, retrenching some innovations that were then creeping into them under the notion of form; although at the same time he was the occasion of taking away the liberty of appeals to the Assembly.

But the Lord Howard, who succeeded him (tho' he was himself a man absolutely unskilled in the legal proceedings of England), endeavored to introduce as many of the English forms as he could, being directly opposite to the Lord Culpeper in that point.

After him Sir Edmund Andros when he was governor caused the statutes of England to be allowed for law there, even such statutes as were made of late time since the grant of the last charter.

And lastly, Governor Nicholson, a man unacquainted with all law except that of Morocco, where he learnt the way of governing by force, has endeavored to introduce all the quirks of the English proceedings by the help of some wretched pettifoggers who have had the direction both of his conscience and his understanding.

They have two sorts of courts that differ only in jurisdiction, namely, the general court and the county courts. I don't mention the court of admiralty, of which there is neither judge nor any salary appointed for him; and indeed upon these terms no man of any rank or abilities would care to undertake such a troublesome office. Neither is there the least occasion of any such charge, because their county courts sitting so frequently have hitherto supplied their place; and upon extraordinary occasion of dispatch in maritime affairs, the first justice in commission is authorized by law to call courts out of course to determine them.

The general court is a court held by the governor and Council who by custom are the judges of it in all civil disputes, but in all criminal cases they are made judges by the charter.

This court, as it did from the beginning so it does still, takes cognizance of all causes—criminal, penal, ecclesiastical, and civil. From this court there is no appeal except the thing in demand exceed the value of three hundred pounds sterling; in which case an appeal is allowed to the queen and Council in England and there determined by a committee of the Privy Council called the Lords of Appeals; the like custom being used for all the other plantations. In criminal cases I don't know that there's any appeal from the sentence of this court, but the governor is authorized to pardon persons found guilty of any crime whatsoever except of treason and willful murder, and even in those cases he may reprieve the criminal if the court represent him to be an object of mercy; which reprieve stands good and may be continued until her Majesty's pleasure be signified therein.

This court is held twice a year, beginning on the 15th of April and on the 15th of October. Each time it continues eighteen days, excluding Sundays, if the business hold them so long. And these are the only times of jail delivery.

The officers attending this court are the sheriff of the county wherein it sits and his under-officers. Their business is to call the litigants and the evidences into court and to impanel juries. But each sheriff in his respective county makes arrests and returns the writs to this court.

The way of impaneling juries to serve in this court is thus: The sheriff and his deputies every morning that the court sits goes about the town summoning the best of the gentlemen who resort thither from all parts of the country. The condition of this summons is that they attend the court that day to serve upon the jury (it not being known whether there will be occasion or no), and if any cause happen to require a jury they are then sworn to try the issue, otherwise they are in the evening, of course, dismissed from all further attendance, though they be not formally discharged by the court. By this means are procured the best juries this country can afford, for if they should be summoned by writ of venire from any particular county, that county cannot afford so many qualified persons as are here to be found because of the great resort of gentlemen from all parts of the colony to these courts as well to see fashions as to dispatch their particular business. Nor is visinage necessary there to distinguish the several customs of particular places, the whole country being as one neighborhood and having the same tenures of land, usages, and customs.

In criminal matters this method is a little altered, because a knowledge of the life and conversation of the party may give light to the jury in their verdict. For this reason a writ of venire issues in such cases to summon six of the nearest neighbors to the criminal, who must be of the same county wherein he lived; which writ is returned by the sheriff of the respective county to the secretary's office, and the names are taken from thence by the sheriff attending the general court and put in the front of the panel, which is filled up with the names of the other gentlemen summoned in the town to be of the petty jury for the trial of that criminal. If the prisoner have a mind to challenge the jurors, the same liberty is allowed him there as in England; and if the panel fall short by reason of such challenge, it must then be made up of the bystanders.

All actions are in that country brought to a determination the third court at farthest unless some special extraordinary reason be shown why the party can't make his defense so soon. The course is thus: Upon the defendant's nonappearance, order goes against the bail (for a *capias* is always their first process) on condition that unless the defendant appear and plead at the next court judgment shall then be awarded for the plaintiff. When the defendant comes to the next court he is held to plead, and if his plea be dilatory and overruled, he is held to plead over immediately. And if it can be the merits are tried that court, but the next it is ended without fail, except something happen to make it highly unreasonable. Thus a year and half ends a cause in the general court and three months in the county court. If anyone appeal from the judgment of the county court, the trial always comes on the succeeding general court, so that all business begun in the county court, tho' it runs to the utmost of the law (without some extraordinary event), is finished in nine months.

Everyone that pleases may plead his own cause or else his friends for him, there being no restraint in that case nor any licensed practitioners in the law. If anyone be dissatisfied with the judgment of the county court, let it be for any sum, little or great, he may have an appeal to the next general court, giving security to answer and abide the judgment of that court. But an action cannot originally be brought in the general court under the value of ten pounds sterling or of two thousand pounds of tobacco.

The county courts are constituted by commission from the governor with advice of Council. They consist of eight or more gentlemen of the county called justices of the peace, the sheriff being only a ministerial officer. This court is held monthly and has jurisdiction of all causes within the county not touching life or member, but in the case of hog stealing they may sentence the criminal to lose his ears, which is allowed by a particular act for that purpose. In all things they proceed in the same manner as the general court.

Besides this monthly court there is a day appointed to be kept annually by the justices of the said court for the care of all orphans and of their estates, and for the binding out and well ordering of such fatherless children who are either without any estate or have very little.

At these courts they inquire into the keeping and management of the orphan as to his sustenance and education. They examine into his estate and the securities thereof—if the sureties continue to be responsible, if his lands and plantations be kept improving and in repair, etc. If the poor orphan be bound an apprentice to any trade, then their business is to inquire how he is kept to his schooling and trade; and if the court find he is either misused or untaught they take him from that master and put him to another of the same trade or of any other trade which they judge best for the child.

Another charitable method in favor of the poor orphans there is this: That besides their trade and schooling the masters are generally obliged to give them at their freedom cattle, tools, or other things to the value of five, six, or ten pounds, according to the age of the child when bound, over and above the usual quantity of corn and clothes. The boys are bound till one and twenty years of age and the girls till eighteen. At which time they who have taken any care to improve themselves generally get well married and live in plenty, tho' they had not a farthing of paternal estate.

Though these courts be yearly appointed for that use, yet the justices do not fail every county court, as occasions happen, to do everything that can be for the benefit of orphans. And this annual court seems to be only a review of their year's work or a retrospection into the observance of their former orders.

7

Of the Church and Church Affairs

Their parishes are accounted large or small in proportion to the number of tithables contained in them and not according to the extent of land. They have in each parish a convenient church built either of timber, brick, or stone, and decently adorned with everything necessary for the celebration of divine service.

If a parish be of greater extent than ordinary, it hath generally a chapel of ease, and some of the parishes have two such chapels besides the church for the greater convenience of the parishioners. In these chapels the minister preaches alternately, always leaving a reader to read prayers and homily when he can't attend himself.

The people are generally of the Church of England, which is the religion established by law in that country, from which there are very few dissenters. Yet liberty of conscience is given to all other congregations pretending to Christianity on condition they submit to all parish duties. They have no more than five conventicles amongst them, namely, three small meetings of Quakers and two of Presbyterians. 'Tis observed that those counties where the Presbyterian meetings are produce very mean tobacco and for that reason can't get an orthodox minister to stay amongst them, but whenever they could the people very orderly went to church. As for the Quakers, 'tis observed by letting them alone they decrease daily.

The maintenance for a minister there is appointed by law at sixteen thousand pounds of tobacco per annum (be the parish great or small) as also a dwelling house and glebe, together with certain perquisites for marriages and funeral sermons. That which makes the difference in the benefices of the clergy is the value of the tobacco according to the distinct species of it or according to the place of its growth. Besides, in large and rich parishes more marriages will probably happen and more funeral sermons.

The fee by law for a funeral sermon is forty shillings or four hundred pounds of tobacco; for a marriage by license twenty shillings or two hundred pounds of tobacco, and where the banns are proclaimed only five shillings or fifty pounds of tobacco.

When these salaries were granted the Assembly valued tobacco at ten shillings per hundred, at which rate the sixteen thousand pounds comes to fourscore pounds sterling. But in all parishes where the sweet-scented grows it has generally been sold of late for near double that value and never under.

In some parishes likewise there are stocks of cattle and Negroes on the glebes which are also allowed to the minister for his use and encouragement, he only being accountable for the surrender of the same value when he leaves the parish.

For the well-governing of these and all other parochial affairs, a vestry is appointed in each parish. These vestries consist of twelve gentlemen of the parish and were first chosen by the vote of the parishioners, but upon the death of one have been continued by the survivors electing another in his place. These are the patrons of the church, and in the name of the parish have the presentation of ministers as well as the sole power of all parish assessments. They are qualified for this employment by subscribing to be conformable to the doctrine and discipline of the Church of England. If there be a minister incumbent, he is always chief of the vestry.

For the ease of the vestry in general and for discharging the business of the parish, they choose two from among themselves to be church wardens, which must be annually changed, that the burden may lie equally upon all. The business of these church wardens is to see the orders and agreements of the vestry performed, to collect all the parish tobaccos and distribute them to the several claimants, to make up the accounts of the parish, and to present all profaneness and immorality.

By these the tobacco of the minister is collected and brought home to him in hogsheads convenient for shipping so that he is at no further trouble but to receive it in that condition. This was ordained by the law of the country for the ease of the ministers that so they being delivered from the trouble of gathering in their dues may have the more time to apply themselves to the exercises of their holy function and live in a decency suitable to their order. It may here be observed that the labor of a dozen Negroes does but answer this salary and seldom yields a greater crop of sweet-scented tobacco than is allowed to each of their ministers.

Probates of wills and administrations are according to their law grantable by the county courts, but the commission must be signed by the governor without fee. Marriage licenses are issued by the clerks of those courts and signed by the first justice in commission or by any other person deputed by the governor, for which a fee of twenty shillings must be paid to the governor. The power of induction upon presentation of ministers is also by their law lodged in the governor's hands. All which acts are contained in the first revisal of their laws, since which her Majesty and her royal predecessors have always been pleased to give an instruction to their governors to that purpose.

In the year 1642, when the sectaries began to spread themselves so much in England, the Assembly made a law against them to prevent their preaching and propagating their doctrines in that colony. They admitted none to preach in their churches but ministers ordained by some reverend bishop of the Church of England; and the governor for the time being, as the most suitable public person among them, was left sole judge of the certificates of such ordination, and so he has continued ever since.

The only thing I have heard the clergy complain of there is what they call precariousness in their livings. That is, they have not inductions generally and therefore are not entitled to a freehold, but are liable without trial or crime alleged to to be put out by the vestry. And though some have prevailed with their vestries to present them for induction, yet the greater number of the ministers have no induction but are entertained from year to year or for term of years by agreement with their vestries. Yet are they very rarely turned out without some great provocation, and then if they have not been abominably scandalous they immediately get other parishes. For there is no benefice whatsoever in that country that remains without a parson if they can get one, and no qualified minister ever yet returned from that country for want of preferment. They have now about a dozen vacant parishes.

8

Concerning the College

The College, as has been hinted, was founded by their late Majesties King William and Queen Mary of happy memory, in the year 1692; towards the founding of which they gave £1,985 14s. 10d. They gave, moreover, towards the endowment of it twenty thousand acres of land, the revenue of 1d. per pound on tobacco exported to the plantations from Virginia and Maryland, and the surveyor general's place of that colony (then void), and appointed them also a burgess to represent them in the Assemblies. The land hitherto has yielded little or no profit. The duty of 1d. per pound brings in about two hundred pounds a year, and the surveyor general's place about fifty pounds a year; to which the Assembly has added a duty on skins and furs exported worth about a hundred pounds a year.

By the same character likewise, their Majesties granted a power to certain gentlemen and the survivors of them as trustees to build and stablish the College by the name of William and Mary College—to consist of a president and six masters or professors and a hundred scholars, more or less (graduates or nongraduates), enabling the said trustees as a body corporate to enjoy annuities spiritual and temporal of the value of £2,000 sterling per annum, with proviso to convert it to the building and adorning the College; and then to make over the remainder to the president and masters and their successors who are likewise to become a corporation and be enabled to purchase and hold to the value of £2,000 a year but no more.

The persons named in the charter for trustees are made governors and visitors of the College and to have a perpetual succession by the name of governors and visitors, with power to fill up their own vacancies happening by the death or removal of any of them. Their complete number may be eighteen but not to exceed twenty, of which one is to be rector and annually chosen by themselves on the first Monday after the 25th of March.

These have the nomination of the president and masters of the College and all other officers belonging to it, and the power of making statutes and ordinances for the better rule and government thereof.

The building is to consist of a quadrangle, two sides of which are yet only carried up. In this part are already finished all conveniences of cooking, brewing, baking, etc., and convenient rooms for the reception of the president and masters, with many more scholars than are as yet come to it. In this part are also the hall and schoolroom.

When the last governor was removed, which was before any room was finished in the College and the boys were taught by the college master in a little schoolhouse close by it, it had more scholars than it has now. Which misfortune has happened by reason of the late confusion occasioned by the furious proceedings of the present governor, so that many chose to send their sons to England and others to keep theirs at home rather than put them to the hazard of being harassed and living in the combustion which that gentleman makes among them.

The method of teaching is likewise very much impaired by the chief master's minding his country affairs. For by this means he is obliged to live several miles from the College upon his own plantation, so that he cannot give that attendance and application which was designed by appointing so good a salary as £100 per annum besides perquisites.

The College revenue is behind hand and the Maryland duty of 1*d.* per pound has not been paid in of late, so that several of the established salaries are in arrear.

9

Of the Militia
in Virginia

The militia are the only standing forces in Virginia. They have no fortress nor so much as any cannon fit for service. Neither are any of these made use of except six small pieces that formerly were mounted on the fort at Jamestown; but these are now removed to Williamsburg where they are of no use but to fire upon some joyful occasions. They are happy in the enjoyment of an everlasting peace, which their poverty and want of towns secure to them. They have the Indians round about in subjection and have no sort of apprehension from them. And for a foreign enemy it can never be worth their while to carry troops sufficient to conquer the country, for the scattering method of their settlement will not answer the charge of an expedition to plunder them. So that they feel none but the distant effects of war which, however, keep 'em so poor that they can boast of nothing but the security of their persons and habitations. They fear no other enemy but only now and then an insolent and oppressive governor who is pleased to abuse the queen's authority by perverting it into arbitrary power and to exasperate the people by their barbarous treatment.

The governor is lieutenant general by his commission and in each county does appoint the colonel, lieutenant colonel, and major, who have under them captains and other commissioned and subaltern officers.

Every freeman (by which denomination they call all but indented or bought servants) from sixteen to sixty years of age is listed in the militia, which by a law is to be mustered in a general muster for each county once a year and in single troops and companies three or four times more; and the most convenient situation for each troop and company is appointed for them to be exercised in. The people there are very skillful in the use of firearms, being all their lives accustomed to shoot in the woods. This, together with a little exercising, would soon make the militia little inferior to regular troops.

The number of the militia is 2,363 lighthorse and 7,159 foot and dragoons; but as very few of the planters are without horses to ride on, so great part of them may easily be made into dragoons if occasion should require.

Instead of the soldiers they formerly kept constantly on foot under the name of rangers to scour the frontiers clear of the Indian enemy, they have lately appointed the militia to march out upon such occasions under the command of the chief officer of the county where this shall be necessary. And if they upon such expedition remain in arms three days and upwards, they are then entitled to pay for the whole time; but if it prove a false alarm and they have no occasion to continue out so long, they can demand nothing.

The number of soldiers in each troop of lighthorse and dragoons are from thirty to forty, as the convenience of the county will admit of the division, and in a company of foot about fifty. The present governor has reduced 'em to this, whereas formerly a troop of horse consisted of fifty and upwards, and a company of foot of seventy effective men. A troop or company may be got together in less than a day's warning.

10

Of the Servants and Slaves
in Virginia

Their servants they distinguish by the names of slaves for life and servants for a time.

Slaves are the Negroes and their posterity following the condition of the mother, according to the maxim *partus sequitur ventrem*. They are called slaves in respect of the time of their servitude because it is for life.

Servants are those which serve only for a few years, according to the time of their indenture or the custom of the country. The custom of the country takes place upon such as have no indentures. The law in this case is that if such servants be under nineteen years of age, they must be brought into court to have their age adjudged, and from the age they are judged to be of they must serve until they reach four and twenty. But if they be adjudged upwards of nineteen, they are then only to be servants for the term of five years.

The male servants and slaves of both sexes are employed together in tilling and manuring the ground, in sowing and planting tobacco, corn, etc. Some distinction, indeed, is made between them in their clothes and food, but the work of both is no other than what the overseers, the freemen, and the planters themselves do.

Sufficient distinction is also made between the female servants and slaves, for a white woman is rarely or never put to work in the ground if she be good for anything else. And to discourage all planters from using any women so, their law imposes the heaviest taxes upon female servants working in the ground, while it suffers all other white women to be absolutely exempted. Whereas on the other hand, it is a common thing to work a woman slave out of doors; nor does the law make any distinction in her taxes, whether her work be abroad or at home.

Because I have heard how strangely cruel and severe the service of this country is represented in some parts of England, I can't forbear affirming that the work of their servants and slaves is no other than what every common freeman does. Neither is any servant required to do more in a day than his overseer. And I can assure you with a great deal of truth that generally their slaves are not worked near so hard nor so many hours in a day as the husbandmen and day laborers in England. An overseer is a man that having served his time has acquired the skill and character of an experienced planter and is therefore entrusted with the direction of the servants and slaves.

But to complete this account of servants I shall give you a short relation of the care their laws take that they be used as tenderly as possible.

By the Laws of Their Country

1. All servants whatsoever have their complaints heard without fee or reward, but if the master be found faulty the charge of the complaint is cast upon him, otherwise the business is done *ex officio*.

2. Any justice of peace may receive the complaint of a servant and order everything relating thereto till the next county court, where it will be finally determined.

3. All masters are under the correction and censure of the county courts to provide for their servants good and wholesome diet, clothing, and lodging.

4. They are always to appear upon the first notice given of the complaint of their servants, otherwise to forfeit the service of them until they do appear.

5. All servants' complaints are to be received at any time in court without process and shall not be delayed for want of form. But the merits of the complaint must be immediately inquired into by the justices, and if the master cause any delay therein the court may remove such servants if they see cause until the master will come to trial.

6. If a master shall at any time disobey an order of court made upon any complaint of a servant, the court is empowered to remove such servant forthwith to another master who will be kinder, giving to the former master the produce only (after fees deducted) of what such servants shall be sold for by public outcry.

7. If a master should be so cruel as to use his servant ill that is fallen sick or lame in his service and thereby rendered unfit for

labor, he must be removed by the church wardens out of the way of such cruelty and boarded in some good planter's house till the time of his freedom, the charge of which must be laid before the next county court, which has power to levy the same from time to time upon the goods and chattels of the master. After which the charge of such boarding is to come upon the parish in general.

8. All hired servants are entitled to these privileges.

9. No master of a servant can make a new bargain for service or other matter with his servant without the privity and consent of a justice of peace, to prevent the master's overreaching or scaring such servant into an unreasonable compliance.

10. The property of all money and goods sent over thither to servants, or carried in with them, is reserved to themselves and remain entirely at their disposal.

11. Each servant at his freedom receives of his master fifteen bushels of corn (which is sufficient for a whole year) and two new suits of clothes, both linen and woolen, and then becomes as free in all respects and as much entitled to the liberties and privileges of the country as any other of the inhabitants or natives are.

12. Each servant has then also a right to take up fifty acres of land, where he can find any unpatented; but that is no great privilege, for anyone may have as good a right for a piece of eight.

This is what the laws prescribe in favor of servants, by which you may find that the cruelties and severities imputed to that country are an unjust reflection. For no people more abhor the thoughts of such usage than the Virginians, nor take more precaution to prevent it.

11

Of the Other Public Charitable Works and Particularly Their Provision for the Poor

They live in so happy a climate and have so fertile a soil that nobody is poor enough to beg or want food, though they have abundance of people that are lazy enough to deserve it. I remember the time when five pound was left by a charitable testator to the poor of the parish he lived in, and it lay nine years before the executors could find one poor enough to be entitled to any part of this legacy; and at last it was all given to one old woman. So that this may in truth be termed the best poor man's country in the world. But as they have nobody that is poor to beggary, so they have few that are rich, because their goods are so heavily burdened with duties in England that they seldom can make any advantage of 'em.

When it happens that by accident or sickness any person is disabled from working and so is forced to depend upon the alms of the parish, he is then very well provided for, not at the common rate of some countries that give but sufficient to preserve the poor from perishing, but the unhappy creature is received into some charitable planter's house where he is at the public charge boarded very plentifully.

Many when they are very aged or by long sickness become poor will sometimes ask to be free from levies and taxes, but very few do ever ask for the parish alms or indeed so much as stand in need of them.

There are large tracts of land, houses, and other things granted to free schools for the education of children in many parts of the country, and some of these are so large that of themselves they are a handsome maintenance to a master; but the additional allowance which gentlemen give with their sons render them a comfortable subsistence. These schools have been founded by the legacies of well inclined gentlemen, and the management of them hath commonly been left to the direction of the county court or to the vestry of the respective parishes, and I have never heard that any of those pious uses have been misapplied. In all other places where such endowments have not been already made the people join and build schools for their children where they may learn upon very easy terms.

12

Of the Tenure by Which They Hold Their Lands and of Their Grants

The tenure of their land there is free and common socage according to custom of East Greenwich and is created by letters patents issuing under the seal of the colony and under the test of the governor-in-chief for the time being; and I don't find that the name of any other officers is necessary to make the patent valid, but it must be granted by consent of Council.

There are three ways of obtaining from her Majesty a title to land there; viz., first, by right and survey; second, by petition for land lapsed; third, by petition for land escheated. The conditions of the two former are the entry of rights, the condition of the third a composition of two pounds of tobacco for every acre.

A right is the title anyone hath by the royal charter to fifty acres of land in consideration of his personal transportation into that country to settle and remain there. By this rule also a man that removes his family is entitled to the same number of acres for his wife and each of his children.

A patent for land upon survey is acquired thus: First the man proves his rights; that is, he makes oath in court of the importation of so many persons with a list of their names. This list is then certified by the clerk of that court to the clerk of the secretary's office who examines into the validity of them and files them in that office, attesting them to be regular. When the rights are thus certified, they are produced to the surveyor of the county and the land is showed to him, who thereupon is bound by his oath to make the survey if the land had been not patented before. These rights to land are as commonly sold by one man to another as the land itself, so that anyone not having rights by his own importation may have them by purchase.

It is the business of the surveyor also to take care that the bounds of his survey be plainly marked either by natural boundaries or else by chopping notches in the trees that happen in the lines of his courses. But this is done at the charge of the man that employs him.

This survey being made, a copy thereof is carried with the certificate of rights to the secretary's office, and there (if there be no objection) a patent must of course be made out upon it which is presented to the governor and Council for them to pass—the patentee having no more to do but to send for it when it is perfected and to pay the fee at the first crop to the sheriff of the county by whom annually the fees are collected.

This patent gives an estate in fee simple upon condition of paying a quitrent of 12*d*. for every fifty acres and of planting or seating thereon within three years according to their law—that is, to clear, plant, and tend an acre of ground with corn, or to build a house and keep a stock of cattle for one whole year together upon the land, after which 'tis presumed they will continue the settlement and not let the stock be lost, which after it has got a taste of those new plantations will never afterwards without confinement remain at an old one. I know that a certain grave author [Charles Davenant, author of *Discourses on the Publick Revenues, And on the Trade of England*] of much learning and little knowledge of the plantations ridicules this law in his *Discourses on the Trade of England*, part 2, page 236. But I believe if he had land there under the conditions of that law he would not, with all his skill in shifting, be able either to avoid paying the quitrents or to continue his right by erecting a hut of bark, as he calls it. This adventrous gentleman has several unjust reflections upon that country, but I impute them all to his writing wholly in favor of the proprietary government and upon other people's information who know as little of the matter as himself.

Lapsed land is when anyone having obtained a patent as before doth not seat or plant thereon within three years as the condition of the patent requires but leaves it still altogether uninhabited and uncultivated. In such case it is said to be lapsed, and any man is at liberty to obtain a new patent of it in his own name. The method of acquiring which patent is thus:

The party must apply himself by petition to the general court, setting forth all the circumstances of the lapse. If this petition is allowed, the court makes an order that a patent be prepared for the petitioner upon the same condition of seating or planting within three years, as was in the former patent. Thus land may be lapsed or lost several times by the negligence of the patentees, who by such omission lose not only the land but all their rights and charges into the bargain.

But if within the three years after the date of the patent the patentee shall seat or plant the said land as the law directs, it cannot afterwards be forfeited but by attainder or escheat, in which case it returns to her Majesty again.

When land is supposed to escheat, the governor issues his warrant to the escheator to make inquest thereof. And when upon such inquest office is found for the queen, it must be recorded in the secretary's office and there kept nine months to see if any person will lay claim to it or can traverse the escheat. If any such appear, upon his petition to the general court he is heard before any grant can be made. If no person oppose the inquest, the land is given to the man that shows the best equitable right thereto, and if there be none such it is then granted to anyone that the governor and Council shall think fit, the grantee always paying two pounds of tobacco per acre into the treasury of the country as a fine of composition with her Majesty for her escheat. And thereupon a patent issues reciting the premises.

13

Of the Liberties and
Naturalization of Aliens
in Virginia

Christians of all nations have equal freedom there, and upon their arrival become *ipso facto* entitled to all the liberties and privileges of the country provided they take the oaths of obedience to the Crown and government.

The method of obtaining naturalization is thus: The party desiring it goes before the governor and tenders his oath of allegiance, which the governor thereupon administers and immediately makes certificate of it under the seal of the colony. By this means the person alien is completely naturalized to all intents and purposes.

All the French refugees sent in thither by the charitable exhibition of his late Majesty King William are naturalized.

In the year 1699 there went over about three hundred of these, and the year following about two hundred more, and so on, till there arrived in all between seven and eight hundred men, women, and children who had fled from France on account of their religion.

Those who went over the first year were advised to seat on a piece of very rich land about twenty miles above the falls of James River on the south side of the river, which land was formerly the seat of a great and warlike nation of Indians called the Monacans, none of which are now left in those parts; but the land still retains their name and is called the Monacan Town.

The refugees that arrived the second year went also first to the Monacan Town, but afterwards upon some disagreement several dispersed themselves up and down the country. And those that have arrived since have followed their example, except some few that settled likewise at the Monacan Town.

The Assembly was very bountiful to those who remained at this town, bestowing on them large donations, money, and provisions for their support. They likewise freed them from every public tax for several years to come and addressed the governor to grant them a brief to entitle them to the charity of all well disposed persons throughout the country, which together with the king's benevolence supported them very comfortably till they could sufficiently supply themselves with necessaries, which now they do indifferently well and begin to have stocks of cattle which are said to give abundantly more milk than any other in the country. I have heard that these people are upon a design of getting into the breed of buffaloes, to which end they lie in wait for their calves that they may tame and raise a stock of them. In which if they succeed 'twill in all probability be greatly for their advantage, for these are much larger than other cattle and have the benefit of being natural to the climate.

They now make many of their own clothes and are resolved as soon as they have improved that manufacture to apply themselves to the making of wine and brandy, which they do not doubt to bring to perfection.

The last year they began an essay of wine, which they made of the wild grapes gathered in the woods, the effect of which was noble strong-bodied claret of a curious flavor. I heard a gentleman who tasted it give it great commendation. Now, if such may be made of the wild vine in the woods, without pruning, weeding, or removing it out of the shade, what may not be produced from a vineyard skillfully cultivated?

I must not here omit doing justice to the goodness and generosity of Colonel Byrd towards these distressed Huguenots. Upon their
first arrival in that country he received them with all the tenderness
of a father, and ever since has constantly given them the utmost
assistance. He not only relieves them but, with a charity very uncommon, is fond of doing it. He makes them the object of his particular care, employing all his skill, and all his friends to advance
their interest both publicly and privately. He spares no expense,
and what is more than that he refuses no trouble for their encouragement. What liberties has he not all along allowed them upon
his own plantations to furnish themselves from thence with corn
and other necessaries? His mills have been at their service to grind
their corn toll-free, and his people are ordered upon all occasions
to assist them. How kind has he been in procuring them contributions from other people? With what zeal did he represent their
cause to the Assembly? And with what earnestness did he press all
his friends in their favor who otherwise told him they could not
have believed their case to be as he related it? For even poverty in
all its distress could not guard them from ill reports, which would
have had a severe effect upon them had they not been protected
by the interest and credit of this honorable gentleman. With what
delight did he afterwards gather in the benevolence that was given?
How frequently does he continue still to visit their families and
with what importunity does he press them to make their wants
known to him that takes pleasure in relieving them? It is easy to
imagine how necessary to an infant settlement are the assistances
of so generous a friend. When several hundred families of men,
women, and children are set ashore naked and hungry in a strange
land, they have not only necessity to struggle with but likewise
with the envy of ill-natured people who fancy they come to eat the
bread out of their mouths. All these difficulties befell these poor
refugees at their first arrival there; but God Almighty raised up
this gentleman not only to succor them with his own charity but
to solicit the liberalities of other people. By these helps they have
hitherto subsisted and been put into some condition to shift for
themselves. However, they are not yet so far advanced but that
their patron may still have an opportunity of showing his kindness
towards them, which is to prevail with the Assembly to bestow

upon them a certain title to the land they now possess, to which as yet they have no other right but the bare sitting down upon unseated land. This seems to be worthy of an early care, lest the land which they have improved by their industry from wild woods should hereafter unjustly be taken away from their children.

14

Of the Currency and Valuation of Coins in Virginia

The coin which chiefly they have among 'em is either gold of the stamp of Arabia or silver and gold of the stamp of the Spanish America. But they have now very little money there and are still like to have rather less than more while matters remain in the ill condition they are. For while they are forbid raising the coin, and the neighboring governments all around are allowed to enhance the rate of it with them to above thirty per cent more than the intrinsic value, all their money will be carried thither, which seems to be the greatest hardship in the world upon that colony. It were much to be wished that all the colonies of the continent under the dominion of England were obliged to have one and the same standard for their coin, that so one government might not suffer by the unreasonable advances of another. The inconveniences to Virginia by the drawing away all the specie are inexpressible, for people want money for traveling expenses, and for paying the small jobs of laborers and artificers who would otherwise save abundance of time to themselves, which is now lost in looking after trivial debts, besides the disadvantage of not being able to turn the penny. By having no ready money many lawsuits commence to demand those debts which by this means are contracted, besides the being forced to keep a thousand unnecessary accounts.

Spanish pistoles pass current there at 17*s*. 6*d*., Arabian chequins 10*s*., pieces of eight if they weigh 16 penny weight (except of Peru) at 5*s*., French crowns at 5*s*., Peru pieces of eight and Dutch dollars at 4*s*., and all English coin as it goes in England.

PART II

OF THE HUSBANDRY AND IMPROVEMENTS OF VIRGINIA

15

Of the People, Inhabitants of Virginia

I can easily imagine that this as well as all the rest of the plantations was for the most part at first peopled by persons of low circumstances and by such as were willing to seek their fortunes in a foreign country. Nor was it hardly possible it should be otherwise, for 'tis not likely that any man of a plentiful estate should voluntarily abandon a happy certainty to roam after imaginary advantages in a New World. Besides which incertainty he must have proposed to himself to encounter the infinite difficulties and dangers that attend a new settlement. These discouragements were sufficient to terrify any man that could live easy in England from going to provoke his fortune in a strange land.

Those that went over to that country first were chiefly single men who had not the encumbrance of wives and children in England, and if they had they did not expose them to the fatigue and hazard of so long a voyage until they saw how it should fare with themselves. From hence it came to pass that when they were settled there in a comfortable way of subsisting a family they grew sensible of the misfortune of wanting wives, and such as had left wives in England sent for them. But the single men were put to their shifts. They excepted against the Indian women on account of their being pagans, and for fear they should conspire with those of their own nation to destroy their husbands. Under this difficulty they had no hopes but that the plenty in which they lived might invite modest women of small fortunes to go over thither from England. However, they would not receive any but such as could carry sufficient certificate of their modesty and good behavior. Those if they were but moderately qualified in all other respects might depend upon marrying very well in those days without any fortune. Nay, the first planters were so far from expecting money with a woman that 'twas a common thing for them to buy a deserving wife at the price of £100 and make themselves believe they had a hopeful bargain.

But this way of peopling the colony was only at first, for after the advantages of the climate and the fruitfulness of the soil were well known and all the dangers incident to infant settlements were over, people of better condition retired thither with their families, either to increase the estates they had before or else to avoid being persecuted for their principles of religion or government.

Thus in the time of the rebellion in England several good Cavalier families went thither with their effects to escape the tyranny of the usurper. And so again upon the Restoration many people of the opposite party took refuge there to shelter themselves from the king's resentment. But they had not many of these last because that country was famous for holding out the longest for the royal family of any of the English dominions; for which reason the Roundheads went for the most part to New England, as did most of those that in the reign of King Charles II were molested on the account of their religion, though some of these fell likewise to the share of Virginia. As for malefactors condemned to transportation, they have always received very few and for many years last past their laws have been severe against them.

16

Of the Buildings
in Virginia

There are two fine public buildings in this country which are the most magnificent of any in America, one of which is the College before spoken of and the other the capitol or State House, as it was formerly called; that is, the house for convention of the General Assembly, for the setting of the general court, for the meeting of the Council, and for keeping of their several offices.

Not far from this is also built the public prison of the country which is a large and convenient structure with partitions for the different sexes and distinct rooms for petty offenders. To this is also annexed a convenient yard to air the criminals in for preservation of their life and health till the time of their trial.

These are all erected at Middle Plantation, now named Williamsburg, where land is laid out for a new town. The College and capitol are both built of brick and covered with shingle.

The private buildings are of late very much improved, several gentlemen there having built themselves large brick houses of many rooms on a floor and several stories high, as also some stone houses. But they don't covet to make them lofty, having extent enough of ground to build upon, and now and then they are visited by high winds which would incommode a towering fabric. They always contrive to have large rooms that they may be cool in summer. Of late they have made their stories much higher than formerly and their windows large and sashed with crystal glass, and within they adorn their apartments with rich furniture.

All their drudgeries of cookery, washing, dairies, etc., are performed in offices detached from the dwelling houses which by this means are kept more cool and sweet.

Their tobacco houses are all built of wood, as open and airy as is consistent with keeping out the rain; which sort of building is most convenient for the curing of their tobacco.

Their common covering for dwelling houses is shingle, which is an oblong square of cypress or pine wood; but they cover their tobacco houses with thin clapboard. And tho' they have slate enough in some particular parts of the country and as strong clay as can be desired for making of tile, yet they have very few tiled houses. Neither has anyone yet thought it worth his while to dig up the slate, which will hardly be made use of till the carriage there becomes cheaper and more common.

17

Of the Edibles, Potables, and Fuel in Virginia

The families being altogether on country seats they have their glaziers, bakers, butchers, and cooks within themselves. They have a great plenty and variety of provisions for their table, and as for spicery and other things that the country don't produce they have constant supplies of 'em from England. The gentry pretend to have their victuals dressed and served up as nicely as at the best tables in London.

When I come to speak of their cattle, I can't forbear charging my countrymen with exceeding ill husbandry in not providing sufficiently for them all winter, by which means they starve their young cattle or at least stint their growth so that they seldom or never grow so large as they would do if they were well managed. For the humor is there [that] if people can but save the lives of their cattle, tho' they suffer them to be never so poor in the winter, yet they will presently grow fat again in the spring, which they esteem sufficient for their purpose. And this is the occasion that their beef and mutton are seldom or never so large or so fat as in England. And yet with the least feeding imaginable they are put into as good case as can be desired.

But the pork, bacon, and fowls of all sorts, both dunghill fowl and waterfowl, tame and wild, must be allowed to have very much the advantage in their several kinds of those in England.

Their fish is in vast plenty and variety, and extraordinary good in their kind. Beef and pork are commonly sold there from one penny to twopence the pound, their fattest and largest pullets at sixpence apiece, their capons at three or four shillings the dozen, their ducks at eightpence or ninepence apiece, their geese at tenpence or a shilling, their turkey hens at fifteen or eighteen pence, and their turkey cocks at two shillings or half a crown. But oysters and wild fowl are not so dear as the things I have reckoned before, being in their season the cheapest victuals they have. Their deer are commonly sold for eight, ten, or twelve shillings a head, according to the scarcity.

The bread in gentlemen's houses is generally made of wheat, but some rather choose the pone, which is the bread made of Indian meal. Many of the poorer sort of people so little regard the English grain that though they might have it with the least trouble in the world, yet they don't mind to sow the ground because they won't be at the trouble of making a fence particularly for it. And therefore their constant bread is pone, not so called from the Latin *panis* but from the Indian name oppone.

A kitchen garden don't thrive better or faster in any part of the universe than there. They have all the culinary plants that grow in England and in far greater perfection than in England. Besides these they have several roots, herbs, vine fruits, and salate [salad] flowers peculiar to themselves, most of which will neither increase nor grow to perfection in England. These they dish up various ways and find them very delicious sauce to their meats, both roast and boiled, fresh and salt. Such are the red buds, sassafras flowers, cymnels, melons, and potatoes whereof I have spoken at large in the fourth chapter of the second book.

It is said of New England that several plants will not grow there which thrive well in England, such as rue, southernwood, rosemary, bays, and lavender; and that others degenerate and will not continue above a year or two at the most, such as July flowers, fennel, enula campana, clary, and bloodwort. But I don't know any English plant, grain, or fruit that miscarries in Virginia; but most of them better their kinds very much by being sowed or planted there. It was formerly said of the redtop turnip that there in three or four years' time it degenerated into rape, but that happened merely by an error in saving the seed, for now it appears that if they cut off the top of such a turnip that has been kept out of the ground all the winter and plant that top alone without the body of the root it yields a seed which mends the turnip in the next sowing.

Their small drink is either wine and water, beer, milk and water, or water alone. Their richer sort generally brew their small beer with malt, which they have from England, though they have as good barley of their own as any in the world; but for want of the convenience of malt houses the inhabitants take no care to sow it. The poorer sort brew their beer with molasses and bran, with Indian corn malted by drying in a stove, with persimmons dried in cakes and baked, with potatoes, with the green stalks of Indian corn cut small and bruised with pompions, and with the *batates canadensis* or Jerusalem artichoke, which some people plant purposely for that use; but this is the least esteemed of all the sorts before mentioned.

Their strong drink is madeira wine, which is a noble strong wine, and punch made either of rum from the Caribbean islands or brandy distilled from their apples and peaches; besides French brandy, wine, and strong beer, which they have constantly from England.

Their fuel is altogether wood, which every man burns at pleasure, it being no other charge to him than the cutting and carrying it home. In all new grounds it is such an encumbrance that they are forced to burn great heaps of it to rid the land. They have very good pit coal (as is formerly mentioned) in several places of the country, but no man has yet thought it worth his while to make use of them, having wood in plenty and lying more convenient for him.

18

Of the Clothing in Virginia

They have their clothing of all sorts from England, as linen, woolen, silk, hats, and leather. Yet flax and hemp grow nowhere in the world better than there. Their sheep yield a mighty increase and bear good fleeces, but they shear them only to cool them. The mulberry tree, whose leaf is the proper food of the silkworm, grows there like a weed, and silkworms have been observed to thrive extremely and without any hazard. The very furs that their hats are made of perhaps go first from thence, and most of their hides lie and rot or are made use of only for covering dry goods in a leaky house. Indeed, some few hides with much ado are tanned and made into servants' shoes, but at so careless a rate that the planters don't care to buy them if they can get others. And sometimes perhaps a better manager than ordinary will vouchsafe to make a pair of breeches of a deerskin. Nay, they are such abominable ill husbands that tho' their country be overrun with wood, yet they have all their wooden ware from England; their cabinets, chairs, tables, stools, chests, boxes, cartwheels, and all other things, even so much as their bowls and birchen brooms, to the eternal reproach of their laziness.

19

Of the Temperature of the Climate and the Inconveniences Attending It

The natural temperature of the inhabited part of the country is hot and moist, tho' this moisture I take to be occasioned by the abundance of low grounds, marshes, creeks, and rivers which are everywhere among their lower settlements. But more backward in the woods where they are now seating and making new plantations they have abundance of high and dry land where there are only crystal streams of water which flow gently from their springs and divide themselves into innumerable branches to moisten and enrich the adjacent lands.

The country is in a very happy situation between the extremes of heat and cold but inclining rather to the first. Certainly it must be a happy climate, since it is very near of the same latitude with the Land of Promise. Besides, as Judea was full of rivers and branches of rivers, so is Virginia. As that was seated upon a great bay and sea, wherein were all the conveniences for shipping and trade, so is Virginia. Had that fertility of soil? So has Virginia equal to any land in the known world. In fine, if anyone impartially considers all the advantages of this country as nature made it, he must allow it to be as fine a place as any in the universe. But I confess I am ashamed to say anything of its improvements, because I must at the same time reproach my countrymen with a laziness that is unpardonable. If there be any excuse for them in this matter, 'tis the exceeding plenty of good things with which nature has blessed them, for where God Almighty is so merciful as to work for people they never work for themselves.

All the countries in the world seated in or near the latitude of Virginia are esteemed the fruitfullest and pleasantest of all climates; as for example, Canaan, Syria, Persia, great part of India, China, and Japan, the Morea, Spain, Portugal, and the coast of Barbary, none of which differ many degrees of latitude from Virginia. These are reckoned the gardens of the world, while Virginia is unjustly neglected by its own inhabitants and abused by other people.

That which makes this country most unfortunate is that it must submit to receive its character from the mouths not only of unfit but very unequal judges, for all its reproaches happen after this manner.

Many of the merchants and others that go thither from England make no distinction between a cold and a hot country, but wisely go sweltering about in their thick clothes all the summer because they used to do so in their northern climate and then unfairly complain of the heat of the country. They greedily surfeit with their delicious fruits and are guilty of great intemperance through the exceeding generosity of the inhabitants, by which means they fall sick and then unjustly complain of the unhealthiness of the country. In the next place, the sailors for want of towns there are put to the hardship of rolling most of the tobacco a mile or more to the waterside; this splinters their hands sometimes and provokes 'em to curse the country. Such exercise and a bright sun makes them hot, and then they imprudently fall to drinking cold water or perhaps new cider, which in its season they find in every planter's house. Or else they greedily devour all the green fruit and unripe trash they can meet with and so fall into fluxes, fevers, and the bellyache; and then, to spare their own indiscretion, they in their tarpaulin language cry God D——— the country. This is the true state of the case as to the complaints of its being sickly, for by the most impartial observation I can make, if people will be persuaded to be temperate and take due care of themselves, I believe it is as healthy a country as any under heaven; but the extraordinary pleasantness of the weather and the goodness of the fruit lead people into many temptations. The clearness and brightness of the sky add new vigor to their spirits and perfectly remove all splenetic and sullen thoughts. Here they enjoy all the benefit of a warm sun, and by their shady groves are protected from its inconvenience. Here all their senses are entertained with an endless succession of native pleasures. Their eyes are ravished with the beauties of naked nature. Their ears are serenaded with the perpetual murmur of brooks and the thorough bass which the wind plays when it wantons through the trees. The merry birds, too, join their pleasing notes to this rural consort, especially the mock birds, who love society so well that whenever they see mankind they will perch upon a twig very near them and sing the sweetest wild airs in the world. But what is most remarkable in these melodious animals—they will frequently fly at small distances before a traveler warbling out their notes several miles on end, and by their music make a man forget the fatigues of his journey. Their taste is regaled with the most delicious fruits which without art they have in great variety and perfection. And then their smell is refreshed with an eternal fragrancy of flowers and sweets with which nature perfumes and adorns the woods almost the whole year round.

Have you pleasure in a garden? All things thrive in it most surprisingly. You can't walk by a bed of flowers but besides the entertainment of their beauty your eyes will be saluted with the charming colors of the humming bird which revels among the flowers and licks off the dew and honey from their tender leaves, on which it only feeds. Its size is not half so large as an English wren, and its color is a glorious shining mixture of scarlet, green, and gold. Colonel Byrd in his garden, which is the finest in that country, has a summerhouse set round with the Indian honeysuckle, which all the summer is continually full of sweet flowers in which these birds delight exceedingly. Upon these flowers I have seen ten or a dozen of these beautiful creatures together, which sported about me so familiarly that with their little wings they often fanned my face.

On the other side, all the annoyances and inconveniences of the country may fairly be summed up under these three heads—thunder, heat, and troublesome vermin.

I confess in the hottest part of summer they have sometimes very loud and surprising thunder, but rarely any damage happens by it. On the contrary, it is of such advantage to the cooling and refining of the air that it is oftener wished for than feared. But they have no earthquakes, which the Caribbean islands are so much troubled with.

Their heat is very seldom troublesome and then only by the accident of a perfect calm, which happens perhaps two or three times in a year and lasts but a few hours at a time; and even that inconvenience is made easy by cool shades, by open airy rooms, summer houses, arbors, and grottos. But the spring and fall afford as pleasant weather as Mahomet promised in his paradise.

All the troublesome vermin that ever I heard anybody complain of are either frogs, snakes, mosquitoes, chinches, seedticks, or redworms (by some called potato lice). Of all which I shall give an account in their order.

Some people have been so ill informed as to say that Virginia is full of toads, though there never yet was seen one toad in it. The marshes, fens, and watery grounds are indeed full of harmless frogs which do no hurt except by the noise of their croaking notes. But in the upper parts of the country where the land is high and dry they are very scarce. In the swamps and running streams they have frogs of an incredible bigness which are called bullfrogs from the roaring they make. Last year I found one of these near a stream of fresh water of so prodigious a magnitude that when I extended its legs I found the distance betwixt them to be seventeen inches and a half. I am confident six Frenchmen might have made a comfortable meal of its carcass.

Some people in England are startled at the very name of the rattlesnake and fancy every corner of that province so much pestered with them that a man goes in constant danger of his life that walks abroad in the woods. But this is as gross a mistake as most of the other ill reports of this country; for in the first place, this snake is very rarely seen, and when that happens it never does the last mischief unless you offer to disturb it and thereby provoke it to bite in its own defense. But it never fails to give you fair warning by making a noise with its rattle which may be heard at a convenient distance. For my own part, I have traveled the country as much as any man in it of my age, by night and by day, above the inhabitants as well as among them, yet I never see a rattlesnake alive and at liberty in all my life. I have seen them indeed after they have been killed or pent up in boxes to be sent to England. The bite of this viper without some immediate application is certainly death, but remedies are so well known that none of their servants are ignorant of them. I never knew any that had been hurt by these or any other of their snakes, although I have a general knowledge all over the country and have been in every part of it. They have several other snakes which are seen more frequently and have very little or no hurt in them; viz., such as they call black snakes, water snakes, and corn snakes. The black viper snake and the copper-bellied snake are said to be as venomous as the rattlesnake, but they also are as seldom seen. These three poisonous snakes bring forth their young alive, whereas the other three sort lay eggs which are hatched afterwards; and that is the distinction they make, esteeming only those to be venomous which are viviparous. They have likewise the horn snake, so called from a sharp horn it carries in its tail with which it assaults anything that offends it with that force that it will strike its tail into the butt end of a musket from whence it is not able to disengage itself.

All sorts of snakes will charm both birds and squirrels, and the Indians pretend to charm them. Several persons have seen squirrels run down a tree directly into a snake's mouth; they have likewise seen birds fluttering up and down and chattering at these snakes till at last they have dropped down just before them.

Some few years ago I was a bear hunting in the woods above the inhabitants, and having straggled from my companions I was entertained at my return with the relation of a pleasant rencounter between a dog and rattlesnake about a squirrel. The snake had got the head and shoulders of the squirrel into his mouth, which being something too large for his throat it took him up some time to moisten the fur of the squirrel with his spawl to make it slip down. The dog took this advantage, seized the hinder parts of the squirrel and tugged with all his might. The snake on the other side would not let go his hold for a long time, till at last, fearing he might be bruised by the dog's running away with him, he gave up his prey to the enemy, which he eat; and we eat the snake, which was dainty food.

Mosquitoes are a sort of vermin of less danger but much more troublesome because more frequent. They are a long-tailed gnat, such as are in all fens and low grounds in England, and I think have no other difference from them than the name. Neither are they troubled with 'em anywhere but in their low grounds and marshes. These insects I believe are stronger and continue longer there, by reason of the warm sun, than in England. Whoever is persecuted with them in his house there may get rid of them by this easy remedy: Let him but set open his windows at sunset and shut them again before the twilight be quite shut in and all the mosquitoes in the room will go out at the windows and leave the room clear.

Chinches are a sort of flat bug which lurks in the bedsteads and bedding and disturbs people's rest a-nights. Every neat housewife contrives there by several devices to keep her beds clear of them. But the best way I ever heard effectually to destroy them is by a narrow search among the bedding early in the spring before these vermin begin to nit and run about. For they lie snug all winter and are in the spring large and full of the winter's growth, having all their seed with them, and so they become a fair mark to find, and may with their whole breed be destroyed.

Seedticks and redworms are small insects that annoy people by day as mosquitoes and chinches do by night, but both these keep out of your way if you will keep out of theirs. For seedticks are nowhere to be met with but in the track of cattle, upon which the great ticks fasten and fill their skins so full of blood that they drop off; and wherever they happen to fall they produce a kind of egg which lies about a fortnight before the seedlings are hatched. These seedlings run in swarms up the next blade of grass that lies in their way and then the first thing that brushes that blade of grass gathers off most of these vermin, which stick like burrs upon anything that touches them.

Redworms lie only in old dead trees and rotten logs, and without sitting down upon such a man never meets with them nor at any other season but only in the midst of summer. A little warm water immediately brings off both seedticks and redworms, tho' they lie never so thick upon any part of the body; but without some such remedy they are so small that nothing will lay hold of them but the point of a penknife, needle, or such like. And tho' nothing be done to remove them, yet the itching they occasion goes away after two days.

Their winters are very short and don't continue above three or four months, of which they have seldom thirty days of unpleasant weather, all the rest being blessed with a clear and a bright sun. However, they have very hard frost sometimes, but it rarely lasts above three or four days—that is, till the wind change; for if it blows not between the northeast and northwest points from the cold Appalachian Mountains, they have no frost at all. But these frosts are attended with a serene sky and are otherwise made delightful by the tameness of the wild fowl and other game, which by their incredible numbers afford the pleasantest shooting in the world.

Their rains, except in the depth of winter, are extremely agreeable and refreshing. All the summer long they last but a few hours at a time and sometimes not above half an hour and then immediately succeeds clear sunshine again; but in that short time it rains so powerfully that it quits the debt of a long drought and makes everything green and gay.

I have heard that this country is reproached with sudden and dangerous changes of weather, but that imputation is unjust. For tho' it be true that in the winter when the wind comes over those vast mountains to the northwest, which are supposed to retain mighty magazines of ice and snow, the weather is then very rigorous; yet in spring, summer, and autumn such winds are only cool and pleasant breezes which serve to refresh the air and correct those excesses of heat which the situation would otherwise make that country liable to.

20

Of the Diseases Incident to Virginia

While we are upon the climate and its accidents, it will not be improper to mention the diseases incident to Virginia. Distempers come not there by choking up the spirits with a foggy and thick air, as in some northern climes, nor by a stifling heat that exhales the vigor of those that dwell in a more southerly latitude, but by a willful and foolish indulging themselves in those pleasures which in a warm and fruitful country nature lavishes upon mankind for their happiness and not for their destruction.

Thus I have seen persons impatient of heat lie almost naked upon the cold grass in the shades and there often forgetting themselves fall asleep. Nay, many are so imprudent as to do this in an evening and perhaps lie so all night, when between the dew from heaven and the damps from the earth such impressions are made upon the humors of their body as occasion fatal distempers.

Thus also have I seen persons put into a great heat by excessive action and in the midst of that heat strip off their clothes and expose their open pores to the air. Nay, I have known some mad enough in this hot condition to take huge draughts of cold water or perhaps of milk and water, which they esteem much more cold in operation than water alone.

And thus likewise have I seen several people (especially newcomers) so intemperate in devouring the pleasant fruits that they have fallen into dangerous fluxes and surfeits. These and such like disorders are the chief occasions of their diseases.

The first sickness that any newcomer happens to have there he unfairly calls a seasoning, be it fever, ague, or anything else that his own folly or excesses bring upon him.

Their intermitting fevers as well as their agues are very troublesome if a fit remedy be not applied. But of late the doctors there have made use of the *cortex peruviana* with success and find that it seldom or never fails to remove the fits. The planters, too, have several roots natural to the country which in this case they cry up as infallible. They have the happiness to have very few doctors, and those such as make use only of simple remedies of which their woods afford great plenty. And indeed their distempers are not many and their cures are so generally known that there is not mystery enough to make a trade of physic there as the learned do in other countries, to the great oppression of mankind.

When these damps, colds, and disorders affect the body more gently and do not seize people violently at first, then for want of some timely application (the planters abhorring all physic except in desperate cases) these small disorders are suffered to go on until they grow into a cachexia by which the body is overrun with obstinate scorbutic humors. And this in a more fierce and virulent degree I take to be the yaws.

The gripes is the distemper of the Caribbean islands, not of that country, and seldom gets footing there and then only upon great provocation—namely, an unreasonable use of filthy and unclean drinks. Perhaps, too, it may come by new and unfine cider, perry [fermented drink made from pears], or peach drink, which the people are impatient to drink before they are ready; or by the excessive use of lime juice and foul sugar in punch and flip; or else by the constant drinking of uncorrected beer made of such windy, unwholesome things as some people make use of in brewing.

Thus having fairly reckoned up all the principal inconveniences of the climate and the distempers incident to the country, I shall add a chapter of the recreations and amusements used there and then proceed to the natural benefits they enjoy. After which I shall conclude with some hints concerning their trade and improvements.

21

Of the Recreations and Pastimes Used in Virginia

For their recreation the plantations, orchards, and gardens constantly afford 'em fragrant and delightful walks. In their woods and fields they have an unknown variety of vegetables and other rarities of nature to discover and observe. They have hunting, fishing, and fowling with which they entertain themselves a hundred ways. Here is the most good nature and hospitality practiced in the world, both towards friends and strangers. But the worst of it is this generosity is attended now and then with a little too much intemperance. The neighborhood is at much the same distance as in the country in England, but with this advantage: that all the better sort of people have been abroad and seen the world, by which means they are free from that stiffness and formality which discover more civility than kindness. And besides, the goodness of the roads and the fairness of the weather bring people oftener together.

The Indians, as I have already observed, had in their hunting a way of concealing themselves and coming up to the deer under the blind of a stalking head, in imitation of which many people have taught their horses to stalk it—that is, to walk gently by the huntsman's side to cover him from the sight of the deer. Others cut down trees for the deer to browse upon and lie in wait behind them. Others again set stakes at a certain distance within their fences where the deer have been used to leap over into a field of peas which they love extremely. These stakes they so place as to run into the body of the deer when he pitches, by which means they impale him.

They hunt their hares (which are very numerous) afoot with mongrels or swift dogs which either catch them quickly or force them to hole in a hollow tree, whither all their hares generally trend when they are closely pursued. As soon as they are thus holed and have crawled up into the body of the tree the business is to kindle a fire and smother them with smoke till they let go their hold and fall to the bottom stifled, from whence they take them. If they have a mind to spare their lives, upon turning them loose they will be as fit as ever to hunt at another time, for the mischief done them by the smoke immediately wears off again.

They have another sort of hunting which is very diverting, and that they call vermin hunting. It is performed afoot with small dogs in the night by the light of the moon or stars. Thus in summertime they find abundance of raccoons, opossums, and foxes in the cornfields and about their plantations, but at other times they must go into the woods for them. The method is to go out with three or four dogs, and as soon as they come to the place they bid the dogs seek out and all the company follow immediately. Wherever a dog barks you may depend upon finding the game, and this alarm draws both men and dogs that way. If this sport be in the woods, the game by that time you come near it is perhaps mounted to the top of a high tree, and then they detach a nimble fellow up after it who must have a scuffle with the beast before he can throw it down to the dogs; and then the sport increases to see the vermin encounter those little curs. In this sort of hunting they also carry their great dogs out with them because wolves, bears, panthers, wildcats, and all other beasts of prey are abroad in the night.

For wolves they make traps and set guns baited in the woods, so that when he offers to seize the bait he pulls the trigger and the gun discharges upon him. What Elian and Pliny write of the horses being benumbed in their legs if they tread in the track of a wolf does not hold good here, for I myself and many others have rid full speed after wolves in the woods and have seen live ones taken out of a trap and dragged at a horse's tail; and yet those that followed on horseback have not perceived any of their horses to falter in their pace.

They have many pretty devices besides the gun to take wild turkeys. And among others a friend of mine invented a great trap wherein he at times caught many turkeys, and particularly seventeen at one time, but he could not contrive it so as to let others in after he had entrapped the first flock until they were taken out.

The Indian invention of weirs in fishing is mightily improved by the English, besides which they make use of seines, trolls, casting nets, setting nets, hand fishing, and angling, and in each find abundance of diversion. I have set in the shade at the heads of the rivers angling and spent as much time in taking the fish off the hook as in waiting for their taking it. Like those of the Euxine Sea, they also fish with spilyards, which is a long line staked out in the river and hung with a great many hooks on short strings fastened to the main line about three or four foot asunder. The only difference is our line is supported by stakes, and theirs is buoyed up with gourds.

Their fowling is answerable to their fishing for plenty of game in its proper season, no plantation being so ill stored as to be without a great deal. They have a vast variety of it, several sorts of which I have not yet mentioned—as beaver, otter, squirrels, partridges, pigeons, and an infinite number of small birds, etc.

The admirable economy of the beavers deserves to be particularly remembered. They cohabit in one house, are incorporated in a regular form of government something like monarchy, and have over them a superintendent which the Indians call pericu. He leads them out to their several employments which consist in felling trees, biting off the branches, and cutting them into certain lengths suitable to the business they design them for, all which they perform with their teeth. When this is done, the governor orders several of his subjects to join together and take up one of those logs which they must carry to their house or dam, as occasion requires. He walks in state by them all the while and sees that everyone bears his equal share of the burden, while he bites with his teeth and lashes with his tail those that lag behind and do not lend all their strength. They commonly build their houses in swamps, and then to raise the water to a convenient height they make a dam with logs and a binding sort of clay so firm that though the water runs continually over, it cannot wash it away. Within these dams they enclose water enough to make a pool like a mill pond, and if a mill happen to be built upon the same stream below their dam, the miller in a dry season finds it worth his while to cut it to supply his mill with water. Upon which disaster the beavers are so expert at their work that in one or two nights' time they will repair the breach and make it perfectly whole again. Sometimes they build their houses in a broad marsh where the tide ebbs and flows, and then they make no dam at all. The doors into their houses are underwater. I have been at the demolishing one of these houses that was found in a marsh and was surprised to find it fortified with logs that were six foot long and ten inches through and had been carried at least 150 yards. This house was three stories high and contained five rooms; that is to say, two in the lower and middle stories and but one at the top. These creatures have a great deal of policy and know how to defeat all the subtlety and strategems of the hunter, who seldom can meet with them tho' they are in great numbers all over the country.

There is yet another kind of sport which the young people take great delight in, and that is the hunting of wild horses which they pursue sometimes with dogs and sometimes without. You must know they have many horses foaled in the woods of the uplands that never were in hand and are as shy as any savage creature. These, having no mark upon them, belong to him that first takes them. However, the captor commonly purchases these horses very dear by spoiling better in the pursuit; in which case he has little to make himself amends besides the pleasure of the chase. And very often this is all he has for it, for the wild horses are so swift that 'tis difficult to catch them, and when they are taken 'tis odds but their grease is melted, or else being old they are so sullen that they can't be tamed.

The inhabitants are very courteous to travelers who need no other recommendation but the being human creatures. A stranger has no more to do but to inquire upon the road where any gentleman or good housekeeper lives, and there he may depend upon being received with hospitality. This good nature is so general among their people that the gentry when they go abroad order their principal servant to entertain all visitors with everything the plantation affords. And the poor planters who have but one bed will very often sit up or lie upon a form or couch all night to make room for a weary traveler to repose himself after his journey.

If there happen to be a churl that either out of covetousness or ill nature won't comply with this generous custom, he has a mark of infamy set upon him and is abhorred by all. But I must confess (and am heartily sorry for the occasion) that this good neighborhood has of late been much depraved by the present governor who practices the detestable politics of governing by parties, by which feuds and heart-burnings have been kindled in the minds of the people, and friendship, hospitality, and good neighborhood have been extremely discouraged.

22

Of the Natural Product of Virginia and the Advantages of Their Husbandry

The extreme fruitfulness of that country has been sufficiently shown in the second book, and I think we may justly add that in that particularly it is not exceeded by any other. No seed is sowed there but it thrives, and most plants are improved by being transplanted thither. And yet there's very little improvement made among them nor anything used in traffic but tobacco.

Besides all the natural productions mentioned in the second book, you may take notice that apples from the seed never degenerate into crabs or wildings there but produce the same or better fruit than the mother tree (which is not so in England) and are wonderfully improved by grafting and managing; yet there are few planters that graft at all and much fewer that take any care to get choice fruits.

The fruit trees are wonderfully quick of growth, so that in six or seven years' time from the planting a man may bring an orchard to bear in great plenty, from which he may make store of good cider or distill great quantities of brandy, for the cider is very strong and yields abundance of spirit. Yet they have very few that take any care at all for an orchard. Nay, many that have good orchards are so negligent of them as to let them go to ruin and expose the trees to be torn and barked by the cattle.

Peaches, nectarines, and apricots as well as plums and cherries grow there upon standard trees. They commonly bear in three years from the stone and thrive so exceedingly that they seem to have no need of grafting or inoculating, if anybody would be so good a husband. And truly I never heard of any that did graft either plum, nectarine, peach, or apricot in that country.

Peaches and nectarines I believe to be spontaneous somewhere or other on that continent, for the Indians have and ever had great variety and finer sorts of them than the English. The best sort of these cling to the stone and will not come off clear—which they call plum-nectarines and plum peaches or clingstones. Some of these are twelve or thirteen inches in girth. These sorts of fruits are raised so easily there that some good husbands plant great orchards of them purposely for their hogs, and others make a drink of them which they call mobby, and either drink it as cider or distill it off for brandy. This makes the best spirit next to grapes.

Grapevines of the English stock as well as those of their own production bear most abundantly if they are suffered to run near the ground, and increase very kindly by slipping; yet very few have them at all in their gardens, much less endeavor to improve them by cutting or laying. Indeed, my curiosity the last year caused me to lay some of the white muscadine which came of a stock removed thither from England, and they increased by this method to admiration. I likewise set several slips of the cuttings of the same vine, and the major part of the sets bore grapes in perfection the first year. I remember I had seven full bunches from one of them.

When a single tree happens in clearing the ground to be left standing with a vine upon it open to the sun and air, that vine generally produces as much as four or five others that remain in the woods. I have seen in this case more grapes upon one single vine than would load a London cart. And for all this the people never remove any of them into their gardens but content themselves throughout the whole country with the grapes they find thus wild. Much less can they be expected to attempt the making of wine or brandy from the grape.

The almond, pomegranate, and fig ripen there very well, and yet there are not ten people in the country that have any of them in their gardens, much less endeavor to preserve any of them for future spending or to propagate them to make a trade.

A garden is nowhere sooner made than there, either for fruits or flowers. Tulips from the seed flower the second year at farthest. All sorts of herbs have there a perfection in their flavor beyond what I ever tasted in a more northern climate, and yet they han't many gardens in the country fit to bear that name.

All sorts of English grain thrive and increase there as well as in any other part of the world—as, for example, wheat, barley, oats, rye, peas, rape, etc., and yet they don't make a trade of any of them. Their peas, indeed, are troubled with weevils which eat a hole in them, but this hole does neither damage the seed nor make the peas unfit for boiling. And such as are sowed late and gathered after August are clear of that inconvenience.

It is thought too much for the same man to make the wheat and grind it, bolt it, and bake it himself; and it is too great a charge for every planter who is willing to sow barley to build a malt house and brewhouse too, or else to have no benefit of his barley; nor will it answer if he would be at the charge. These things can never be expected from a single family. But if they had cohabitations it might be thought worth attempting. Neither as they are now settled can they find any certain market for their other grain, which if they had towns would be quite otherwise.

Rice has been tried there and is found to grow as well as in Carolina or in any other part of the earth, but it labors under the same inconvenience—the want of a community to husk and clean it, and, after all, to take it off the planters' hands.

I have related at large in the first book how flax, hemp, cotton, and the silkworms have thriven there in the several essays made upon them; how formerly there was encouragement given for making of linen, silk, etc., and how all persons not performing several things towards producing of them were put under a fine. But now all encouragement of such things is taken away, and people are not only suffered to neglect them, but such as do go about them are discouraged by their governor, according to the maxim laid down in the memorials before recited.

The sheep increase well and bear good fleeces, but they generally are suffered to be torn off their backs by briars and bushes instead of being shorn, or else are left rotting upon the dunghill with their skins.

Bees thrive there abundantly and will very easily yield to the careful housewife two crops of honey in a year and besides lay up a winter store sufficient to preserve their stocks.

The beeves, when any care is taken of them in the winter, come to great perfection. They have noble marshes there which with the charge of draining only would make as fine pastures as any in the world, and yet there is not a hundred acres of marsh drained throughout the whole country.

Hogs swarm like vermin upon the earth and are often accounted such, insomuch that when an inventory of any considerable man's estate is taken by the executors, the hogs are left out and not listed in the appraisement. The hogs run where they list and find their own support in the woods without any care of the owner, and in many plantations it is well if the proprietor can find and catch the pigs or any part of a farrow when they are young to mark them, for if there be any marked in a gang of hogs they determine the property of the rest, because they seldom miss their gangs. But as they are bred in company, so they continue to the end.

The woods produce great variety of incense and sweet gums

which distill from several trees, as also trees bearing honey and sugar as before mentioned. Yet there's no use made of any of them, either for profit or refreshment.

All sorts of naval stores may be produced there, as pitch, tar, rosin, turpentine, plank, timber, and all sorts of masts and yards, besides sails, cordage, and iron, and all these may be transported by an easy water carriage.

These and a thousand other advantages that country naturally affords which its inhabitants make no manner of use of. They can see their naval stores daily benefit other people who send thither to build ships, while they, instead of promoting such undertakings among themselves and easing such as are willing to go upon them, allow them no manner of encouragement, but rather the contrary. They receive no benefit nor refreshment from the sweets and precious things they have growing amongst them, but make use of the industry of England for all such things.

What advantages do they see the neighboring plantations make of their grain and provisions, while they who can produce them infinitely better not only neglect the making a trade thereof but even a necessary provision against an accidental scarcity—contenting themselves with a supply of food from hand to mouth, so that if it should please God to send them an unseasonable year there would not be found in the country provision sufficient to support the people for three months extraordinary.

By reason of the unfortunate method of the settlement and want of cohabitation they cannot make a beneficial use of their flax, hemp, cotton, silk, silkgrass, and wool, which might otherwise supply their necessities, and leave the produce of tobacco to enrich them when a gainful market can be found for it.

Thus they depend altogether upon the liberality of nature without endeavoring to improve its gifts by art or industry. They sponge upon the blessings of a warm sun and a fruitful soil and almost grutch [grudge] the pains of gathering in the bounties of the earth. I should be ashamed to publish this slothful indolence of my countrymen but that I hope it will rouse them out of their lethargy and excite them to make the most of all those happy advantages which nature has given them. And if it does this I am sure they will have the goodness to forgive me.